EVOLUTIONARIES:

Transformational Leadership

The Pocket Book

Randy Harrington, PhD & Carmen E. Voillequé

CHAPTERS

1. Evolutionaries

2. Evolutionary Planning

3. Evolutionary Leadership

4. Evolutionary Communication

5. Evolutionary Teams

6. Evolutionary Innovation

7. Evolutionary Guidance

8. Evolutionary Women

9. The Code of an Evolutionary

10. When Evolutionaries Fail

Acknowledgments

The first person that we want to thank in the writing of this book is you. The fact that you are taking your valuable time to learn new ideas and to be in dialogue with us is a gift. We have thought about you a lot – the hardships, wins, and big dreams that drive you and make you who you are. And we have huge faith in you and what you can accomplish in the world.

And, of course, this book could never have been written without the people who engaged in conversations with us over the last year to provide much of the key wisdom provided in this book: Captain Steve Ahlberg, Chandra Brown, Todd Davidson, Mike Foley, Geoff Gilmore, Cindy Tortorici, and Scott West. They have our highest gratitude!

We thank our clients for teaching us. We have noticed that when we provide the best value to our clients we tend to also learn the most. It has been an honor (and often an adventure) to see the heroic efforts taken in organizations that are fundamentally transforming who they are and what is possible in the world.

We would also like to thank our colleagues Jackson Hataway and JoAnn Edwards for the good wisdom, consistent support, and for always believing in us.

As we wrote this book, we found ourselves returning again and again to share incredible Evolutionary stories and examples provided by the life and work of one friend in particular. While she is not showcased in this book (she needs a whole book dedicated to her alone!) she lives the Evolutionary life better than anyone we know, and continues to be our constant source for inspiration. If we did not have Chief Judge Ann Aiken of the U.S. District Court, District of Oregon, in our lives, this book may never have been written. Thanks, Ann.

And a special thank you for our families, Patty, Cara, Dana and Gwen Harrington; JP and Claire Voillequé; and all of the other people that put up with us.

WARNING:

The act of reading this book is not neutral. By calling attention to this very special group of people you are now a party to their successes and failures. Evolutionaries are everywhere and they are trying to change the world all the time. Once you begin seeing them, you lose your innocence. You are in the game! We hope you are ready.

CHAPTER 1: EVOLUTIONARIES

It is extremely difficult to manifest and sustain strategic clarity in a world where thousands of tasks bog down the days and the rules seem to change the moment we gain momentum. The sad truth is that most organizations are simply trying to reduce the frustration of a beleaguered staff who see winning as surviving, biding time until some external force defines their options and direction for good or ill.

Often it is in times such as these that organizational leaders call us. They know things need to change, and they know they need help, but what they often don't know is what kind of help they are looking for. So, they ask us to come in and "do some training" or "facilitate some planning sessions." But what they are really looking for is a kind of positive organizational transformation. More training is not the solution. And they know it isn't the solution, but there isn't another way to talk about transformative change. We lack a common language to define this sort of transformational organizational need. In this book, we will provide a new way to talk about organizational transformation and through these conversations we believe you can achieve the evolution you are seeking for your team, company, or community.

We offer the term **Evolutionaries** to describe the kind of people that lead organizations through transformative change. We believe these leaders MUST be present within the organization itself – they cannot be outside consultants, advisors or coaches. (Of course, as we are actually consultants ourselves, we still believe that outside facilitators provide a crucial role in organizational transformation – just not as *Evolutionaries*.)

An **Evolutionary** is:

- **A Planner:** Evolutionaries need a cause and a good, flexible plan – they need to be attached to a strategic outcome that they are invested in and believe in.
- **A Leader:** Evolutionaries must know the business at hand and possess the kind of "street credibility" with your organization's people that garners trust, respect and followers.
- **A Communicator:** Evolutionaries are experts at delivering clear and inspiring messages. They can adapt to the language culture of those they lead, and they are willing to learn new "languages" as necessary to facilitate positive transformation for an organization.
- **A Teammate:** Evolutionaries aren't just great leaders, they are great teammates and great followers. In fact, if you don't have a strong desire to be a part of a team, or follow great leadership when you see it, you are probably not an Evolutionary.
- **An Innovator:** Evolutionaries are skilled in the business of predicting the future. They know how to identify trends, seek out thought leadership, and be awake and aware of new opportunities; they are open to change, comfortable with ambiguity and highly adaptable.
- **A Guide:** Evolutionaries are masters in the art and science of Guidance. They are confident in the "trail"; they know how to facilitate, inspire, foster trust, stay

the course and bring people successfully toward a desired end state.

You need Evolutionaries to help you lead your organization in times of transition. They are the secret weapons of organizations that transform quickly, that are able to adapt and innovate, and rise to any challenge, no matter how unexpected. But make no mistake – Evolutionaries are not superheroes; they are not invincible. Nor are they the only type of leader your organization needs. Evolutionaries are not the best people to lead in times of stability and maintenance. Evolutionaries have weaknesses: patience, consistency, and long-term commitment to name a few. But if it is time for a change in your organization, a transformation, or just a new idea, then you are in need of a good Evolutionary.

Special Note:

The chapters in this book are independent. While we think each offers unique lessons, we don't expect you to read them in order. We encourage you to read those most relevant to your needs first, and then explore the others. To help you identify which chapters might benefit you the most, we offer the following assessments designed to diagnose your Evolutionary needs and potential.

Quiz 1: Do You Need an Evolutionary?

Check the boxes YES or NO

QUESTION	YES	NO
1. Do you struggle to see a clear path for growth in your business over the next 5–10 years?		
2. Are you struggling with silos in your organization?		
3. Do you feel there should be more cross-functional collaboration in your organization?		
4. Do you feel like there is too much waste in your organization (funds, resources, time)?		
5. Do people in your organization lack focus or find it hard to define a common vision?		
6. Do you feel like you are reacting to changes in technology instead of being proactive?		
7. Do you wonder what you should be thinking about for future planning?		
8. Are there areas of expertise that you need in your organization, but struggle to synthesize all of the necessary information?		
9. Is it a chore to go to work each day? Do you feel like you are losing steam in your work?		
10. Do you struggle with finding enough professional challenge in your work? Are you bored?		

If you answered "yes" to five or more of the questions above, it is likely that your organization would benefit from a stronger internal Evolutionary presence. In the chapters that follow, we describe how different types of Evolutionaries can serve an organization in times that require significant transformational change. Read on to find out which sort of Evolutionaries your organization needs, how to identify and recruit them, and how to optimize their potential to meet your strategic goals.

QUIZ 2: ARE *YOU* AN EVOLUTIONARY?

For the following statements, assign a numerical value (1–5) based on your level of agreement with the statement. Use the scoring structure provided below.

5 – STRONGLY AGREE 4 – AGREE 3 – NEUTRAL 2 – DISAGREE 1 – STRONGLY DISAGREE

CHANGE

	QUESTION	SCORE
1.	Change is a necessity for organizational growth.	
2.	I often feel like the pace of change in my organization is way too slow.	
3.	I often feel like the pace of change in my organization is way too fast.	
4.	Everything can be improved.	
5.	I like the idea of working on entirely new systems, projects and ideas – things that are unproven.	
6.	I can't help myself from solving problems – even if they are not directly related to my world.	
7.	I frequently work without regard to the clock or "normal" workday rhythms.	

Score: _____/35

PLANNING

	QUESTION	SCORE
8.	I have a reasonably clear sense of what I intend to accomplish in my professional work over the next five years.	
9.	I approach work from a project perspective; planning, executing, completing, and evaluating all along the way.	
10.	I believe planning is critical for success.	
11.	I think it is reasonable to make 20-year strategic plans.	
12.	I believe too much time is spent on planning.	
13.	With so much uncertainty in the world, long-term planning is basically worthless.	
14.	Once I know the strategic outcome, I am easily able to generate plans to meet the goal.	
15.	When I have a good plan, I am more invested in the mission ahead.	
16.	I don't mind focusing on details, if they lead to a better plan.	

Score: _____/45

LEADERSHIP

	QUESTION	SCORE
17.	I feel comfortable in leadership positions.	
18.	I seek opportunities to lead projects.	
19.	When a new project opportunity arises, I volunteer to lead the project.	
20.	Leadership begins with a vision of what is necessary to achieve specific goals.	
21.	Leadership is a natural trait; some people have it and some don't.	
22.	I am very clear about what is important and what is less important in my day-to-day work.	
23.	I know my industry; I have deep experience.	
24.	I know my industry; I have formal training and/or credentials.	
25.	My peers often seek me out for business/professional advice.	
26.	I motivate the people I work with to obtain organizational goals.	

SCORE: _____/50

COMMUNICATION

	QUESTION	SCORE
27.	I like to give speeches and presentations.	
28.	I like to lead meetings.	
29.	People tell me I am a good writer.	
30.	I read more than one book at a time.	
31.	I am a student of the world – ready and able to learn from other traditions and cultures.	
32.	I can tell a good story.	
33.	I can coach other people to improve their communication skills.	
34.	People often come to me for advice on communication issues.	
35.	I enjoy learning new business "languages" and can adapt quickly to new business environments.	
36.	I am able to speak "across the organization" and make connections between departments.	
37.	I proofread my work carefully.	
38.	I believe in the value of practice, rehearsal, and preparation.	

Score: _____/60

TEAMWORK

	QUESTION	SCORE
39.	I value working with others in a team environment.	
40.	Team bonds go beyond the work at hand; teams should be special.	
41.	Real teams can accomplish more than simple groups of people.	
42.	I enjoy competition...and I am competitive.	
43.	Team concepts are overused in the modern corporate environment – they can bog things down.	
44.	Being on a team means checking your ego and being a good follower as well as a good leader.	

Score: _____/30

INNOVATION

	QUESTION	SCORE
45.	I read about all kinds of things that are not directly related to my job.	
46.	I am a natural networker; when I meet people I almost always make connections.	
47.	I read more than five professional magazines or journals every month.	
48.	I spend hours each week working to identify future trends that will affect my organization.	
49.	I intentionally network with people outside my professional circle to better understand best practices from other industries and other points of view.	
50.	I am proud of my accomplishments so far, but I know have much more I can do.	

Score: _____/30

GUIDANCE

	QUESTION	SCORE
51.	I like to help people learn.	
52.	People say I am a good coach/mentor.	
53.	The people I have taught or coached are often promoted and/or recognized for their work.	
54.	I am able to explain complicated ideas in relatively simple and clear language.	
55.	I believe that teaching is one of the most important forms of influence.	
56.	I am a talented facilitator.	
57.	I am able to listen carefully and facilitate group decision-making.	
58.	I am comfortable working with large groups of professionals representing a diversity of professional points of view.	

Score: _____/40

MORAL CODE

	QUESTION	SCORE
59.	I adhere to a clear set of moral and ethical standards.	
60.	I believe I have a responsibility to make the world a better place.	
61.	I am happy to work on efforts that may not come to fruition for several generations.	
62.	I spend active time supporting efforts to help the next generation learn, grow, and be healthy.	
63.	I believe there are fundamental values that are universal.	
64.	I don't think about "retiring"; at some level I always see myself contributing.	
65.	I am driven by inspiration more than a paycheck.	
66.	Business is not just about profit and loss; it is also the place to work on issues like social justice.	
67.	I actively remove myself from people or situations that don't support my core values.	

Score: _____/45

Change Total: _____/35

Planning Total: _____/45

Leadership Total: _____/50

Communication Total: _____/60

Teamwork Total: _____/30

Innovation Total: _____/30

Guidance Total: _____/40

Moral Code Total: _____/45

Evolutionary Degrees Total (Grand Total): _____/335

It may be that you are one of the Evolutionaries that can help to lead your organization forward. Or, it may be that you are interested in increasing your skills by developing your Evolutionary potential. The good news is that Evolutionaries are rarely, if ever, born. These skills can be learned, and are honed over time through conscious attention and application. The quiz you just took will tell you where you fall on what we call the "Evolutionary Development Scale." It will also tell you which areas you are strong and which areas you are weak in your Evolutionary skill set (for example, you may be very strong in Evolutionary Communication skills, but need work in Evolutionary Planning skills). Once you have calculated your score, read the descriptions below to learn where you fall on the Evolutionary Development Scale, and areas you can focus on for improvement.

Evolutionary Degrees:

- Beginner (scores from 65 to 200)
- Apprentice (scores from 201 to 270)
- Guilded (scores from 271 to 325)
- Master (scores from 325 to 335)

It takes time to become an Evolutionary. There are degrees of development. Your quiz score shows you what degree you have already achieved, and now we encourage you to read on for coaching tips you can use as you continue on your Evolutionary path to the next degree of development.

DEGREES OF AN EVOLUTIONARY

Beginner: Because most people are not aware that the Evolutionary path exists, to be a beginner as an Evolutionary is to be a part of a rare group of people. To acknowledge the Evolutionary as a "way to be" is an enormous step all on its own. You see the potential of growth and development in the actions that you take every day. It's not a new course you have to take or seminar you need to attend (though these things can help inform your observations), it is part of your daily life – which is rich with potential for learning and excelling. You are awake to the potential of 24/7 learning and you do not feel daunted by it. You look forward to the changes ahead in your life (especially the challenges), and are eager to learn from them.

Coaching tips:

- Learn how to learn from fiction and popular entertainment. If you watch a movie, think about it from the possibility of transformational change. How might it be used as a conversation starter for your next pitch or conflict at work? Or, consider cutting out a cartoon that made you laugh because it was about the failure to learn or the difficulties of change and post it in your office as a reminder.
- Talk to people and listen to people who have gone through significant change. Ask them what was most helpful? What was least helpful? What was surprising? What would they change about the experience? Begin to see yourself as an anthropologist of the change experience in all sorts of different situations.
- Develop a huge appetite for inquiry. Triple the number of questions you are asking on a regular basis. Learn from the everyday.

Apprentice: To be an apprentice is to formalize your learning through seeking out mentorship and intentionally beginning the quest to develop your Evolutionary skill set. You are identifying and forming formal and informal relationships with teachers of all kinds, both within and outside of your industry. You are reaching beyond your current job duties and seeking knowledge in different areas and how to apply that knowledge in different contexts. You are engaging in a course for "learning how you learn," working to achieve not just depth of experience, but breadth of experience. This can look like volunteering on a project led by someone you admire, learning to play a musical instrument, taking a martial arts class, or even doing community work. The point is that you are taking on these new learning endeavors as an effort to better observe your own development style – what makes you better, and how it works to do so. Knowing this about yourself is a powerful driver in your continued development over the course of your lifetime.

And the same breadth of exposure you apply to seeking out these more formal learning experiences should also apply to the books that you read, your media exposure, the places you travel and the events you attend. Increasing the diversity of people, places, academic literature, media, etc., to which you are exposed allows you not only to discover how you learn, but how you fail, how you persevere, and when necessary, how you redirect your efforts. The more you practice these skills, the more "change-ready," adaptable, confident and self-aware you become. You are increasing your ability to adapt to any situation and any experience and you are learning how to take the change experience in stride, even to anticipate it and look forward to the change.

You also realize that you want to make the world a better place and have thoroughly internalized the importance this mission will have in everything you choose to do from this point forward in your life. You have made a commitment to learning and action that is positive and future-oriented. You are making choices now with a strong *intent*.

Coaching tips:

- Broaden your experience and seek learning opportunities using a three-pronged approach (interpersonal, technical, and experiential). Don't just focus on your technical skills or specific job experience. Look for areas that expand your relationship-building opportunities and self-awareness. Seek out new experiences that challenge you to learn and to fail – that stretch you beyond what is comfortable. It is only in situations of the "unexpected" that we can truly adapt, and Evolutionaries know they must "surprise" themselves in order to develop.

- Test your assumptions about your ability to influence others. For example, consciously take the time to dress more nicely when you go to work or to a social event and carefully observe what sort of reaction you get. How is it different? Or, take time to prepare with more detail for a work presentation and see what kind of feedback you get. Make observations about intentional small changes you make to see if they increase or decrease your ability to influence stakeholders and achieve your goals. Make note of what you learn about your ability to foster change – no matter how small it may seem.

- Set up mini-goals for increasing your breadth of knowledge and experience. Visit a museum you have never been to in your community. Take a pottery class or learn how to dance. Finally read that *War and Peace* novel you have had on your shelf. Listen to the four-hour version of the opera your friend told you about.

Take a digital media course or vow to listen to NPR at least 30 minutes each day. You get the idea...

Guilded: You are Guilded when many of the people who meet you, unprovoked, begin to turn to you, count on you, and assign to you the privileges of thought leadership that come with being an Evolutionary. You are able to legitimately claim the face of a person who is positively future-focused and able to yield results where others would have struggled or failed. You have a history, a track record, of time in your life that demonstrates you have "been there, done that, and succeeded against the odds." You have a legacy of experience, good and bad, that you have the ability to draw on both for professional credibility and for problem solving strategy and technique. *Note: This does not mean that you have gray hair!* Some of the Guilded Evolutionaries we know are quite young. This does not mean that they are smarter than those of us that developed later in life, but it does mean they probably had a head start. Some people began their Evolutionary development as children. Perhaps they were raised in a way that offered highly diverse exposure opportunities and lots of change. Maybe you know a young Evolutionary that was lucky enough to experience several different cultures, classes, countries, languages, and educational programs in their youth. Maybe you worked in a field hospital in Darfur for two years in your early twenties. The point is, many people have taken the accelerated course in "change-readiness" through their unique early life experience.

Whether early in life, or later, the key to becoming an Evolutionary is that you have taken higher risks than most, you have failed more often or more deeply than most, and you know how to overcome failure. You have also achieved formal levels of certification in your field and recognition within the various disciplines that you are pursuing or have pursued in the past. You have racked up achievements in life in general, doing things that most other people have not attempted unless they are exceptionally driven. Finally, you have come to the realization that to really do important things in the world you cannot do it alone. You have come to respect the power of the collectivity and know how to harness that power to achieve future-ready goals. And you are compensated, promoted, and professionally rewarded for this special talent.

Coaching tips:

- Learn how to set expectations with other people so that you are not being unfair to them. It is classic for a Guilded Evolutionary to identify a talent in another person and call it out. It is also likely that talented people will present themselves to you because they recognize your Evolutionary quality. But it is perhaps a downfall of the Evolutionary that he or she tends to see the ultimate potential – the peak possibility – in each person that comes along and not tend to the situational realities, personal limitations, and series of events that may impede the realization of that potential. So, it is important that you don't set false expectations for when and how the Evolutionary work, ideas, innovations and transformation you propose in the team, organization or the world at large will really be done. You need to identify and enlist talented people to assist in your efforts, but be careful not to promise them more than you can deliver. (Evolutionaries have been accused of talking "pie in the sky" more than a time or two!)

- Form unlikely, but successful professional partnerships, even if you are not directly involved with them. Introduce great leaders you know to other top performers. Create synergies between volunteer efforts in your community that you know overlap or share goals. Connect vendors with other companies that might benefit from a partnership. Demonstrate your ability to build connections and bring people and entities together in ways that could never be done without your assistance, even when you and your company are not the beneficiary of the partnerships.

- Seek out long-standing problems that need to be addressed and apply your talent to trying to solve those problems that others find too challenging. Choose these problems carefully – make sure they align with your commitment to building a positive future.

- As an Apprentice Evolutionary your job was to broaden your knowledge and experience. Now, as a Guilded Evolutionary you must begin to narrow your focus. Choose some challenges and problems where you can make a difference in your organization, community and world, and muster the vast resources you have accumulated in your life to tackle the monster issues that you most care about. Figure out the value-driven mission or missions that you will spend the next 10 years of your life working on.

- Be engaged in teaching others. You should spend much more time in "teaching" mode than in "doing" mode on a daily basis. Embrace your role as mentor, coach, and guide to others.

Master: The big shift toward mastery is that you are no longer doing just one job. You have risen above any job description or position and what you do is now *your life*. There is no differentiation between who you are and the many things that you do. This is not the same thing as being a "workaholic," though it can look similar to outsiders. What it means is that you are always operating in the *Evolutionary state of being*. They say the Dalai Lama is always in a state of meditation, he just chooses to adjust or intensify his state over the course of the day to address the present (what is in front of him at the time). Similarly, you also may hold a job title, but as far as you are concerned, you are on a much bigger journey in your work and your life and beyond than what can be detailed in a standard job description. You are focused on impacting things that go well beyond your company and even beyond your own life span. You are thinking about how to make a positive difference that will be relevant and endure for generations. Almost all your time is now devoted to the teaching and guidance of others in all areas of your work and life. But you are also in a perpetual mode of listening and learning. Everything in life is a teaching and learning moment; all experience is adding to the vast and complex tapestry. You no longer have the experience of fear and intimidation around change. You are comfortable and ready for even the most unexpected of circumstances because you live perpetually in an Evolutionary state of being and trust your responses to that change. You are able to accurately judge the ability of an individual or a team to perform at full capacity. (Note: we are rarely able to do any of this well, let alone maintain this level of achievement consistently, which is why it is often identified as "magic" when people see it in action.)

Coaching tips:

- Be careful of your own ego. Repeat over and over the mantra, "It's not about me." You are *facilitating* the development of others, you are not developing them. You are facilitating transformational change in the world, but you are not a "change-maker." Be the master of your ego.
- Be very discerning about the projects that you take on. As a master Evolutionary, you will be offered a flood of opportunities because of your strong problem-solving talent. Just like anyone else, you have a fixed amount of time and resources, and even at maximum capacity you are limited. Just because you *can* do something doesn't mean you *should* do it. Be careful where you choose to devote your time.
- Be constantly reinforcing your own humility. People are going to give you a lot of positive feedback and accolades. But if you start to really need that recognition, it is a problem. Take on learning something totally new each year so you remember what it is like to be "dumb," to fail or to just be inept at something. Let those that admire you watch you learn something new – it is humbling for you, and inspirational for them.

- Realize that what you say and do ripples out beyond your sphere of perception; many people will repeat your words, share your wisdom and relay your ideas to others they know. Your reach is much further than that of the average person. So, you have a more heightened responsibility for your words and actions than others might have. You are more in the public eye than most people, and so it is worse when you violate that public trust.

CHAPTER 2: EVOLUTIONARY PLANNING

Great planning needs to begin with "Why". When you know your organization's reason for being—why it exists—you can begin to plan with confidence, even if you don't know all of the answers and the future is unpredictable. Evolutionaries are naturals when it comes to planning with this big picture focus in mind. In fact, you will know you have an Evolutionary planner in the room when he or she will continually get off track, into deep water, into other people's "turf," and frustrated in planning conversations that foot to closely to short-term goals and the annual budget. There is nothing wrong with having good old-fashioned tactical budget planning conversations and short-term performance indicators. But an Evolutionary planner will become very uncomfortable if that conversation takes the place of a real strategic/Evolutionary plan for your organization.

The Evolutionary planner knows that a good strategic plan has to offer daily, relevant, and easily understandable guidance for thousands of decision points, communications, and actions that cannot be conceptualized or predicted. Good plans have to be both resolute and flexible.

Evolutionary plans are:

- **Short.** They can be read in a single sitting.
- **Simple.** They are easily understandable to people inside of and outside of the organization.
- **Flexible.** They flip the funnel, allowing for more options at the conclusion of each planning phase instead of forcing choices too early.
- **Public.** They are accessible, value-driven, and something you are proud to share.
- **Inclusive.** Everyone in the organization should see themselves in the plan and be responsible for the plan.
- **Factual.** The plan makes use of a wide range of evidence from external empirical data points to informal media clips of customer needs.
- **Common Sense.** They have a "face validity" to them.
- **Emotional.** They evoke allegiance, excitement, and direct action.
- **Art.** They are professionally, artistically presented.

HOW EVOLUTIONARIES PLAN

Evolutionaries accept that plans can change, and they know when to alter a plan to meet the end goal. This often happens in the business world – you plan and as soon as you are done planning, the economic environment changes or new competition moves in and the plan is already obsolete. So, it makes sense to ask: Why even plan? The answer Evolutionaries know is because the way you plan can have a game-changing impact, no matter what may happen in the actual game.

Evolutionaries know that the planning process helps drive commitment to the strategy, even if the plan ends up changing later. What's more, planning together as a team also helps drive confidence in responses to the "what if" situations that will inevitably occur.

Planning really has two parts: there's planning and then there's "now we have the plan..." Evolutionaries are not just skilled in framing the plan; they are skilled in selling the plan and executing on the plan. They can Tarzan between these skills easily – whereas most other people can't.

Evolutionary Planners:

- *Commit to the mission*
- *Master the plan*
- *Are comfortable with ambiguity*
- *Display adaptability*

Evolutionary planners are successful planners because they **commit to the mission** at hand. Buying into the desired end state of the plan may seem like a no-brainer for success, but you might be surprised by how many executives do not really commit to or have a deep belief in the goals they say that they are trying to achieve. We all have trouble buying into our plans when we don't really identify with why we are doing the planning in the first place. Evolutionary planners take the time to discover why they are acting, and this allows them to be confident throughout the planning process. Evolutionaries can easily communicate why the plan is good because they know where the plan is leading and possess a strong belief in the value of the end result.

Evolutionary planners **master the plan**. They know it forwards and backwards, inside out and upside down. They know every nuance and every alternate scenario, every back-up plan and every team substitution. Knowing the plan inside out allows Evolutionaries to be dynamic in using the plan to achieve their mission. By mastering the plan and helping each member of the organization to also master the plan, Evolutionary Planners are able to make extremely difficult decisions for their organization around staffing and structure that might otherwise fracture the culture or shake organizational foundations. No one said transformation was easy – but Evolutionaries know that a good plan can prepare people for the disruption that always comes with change.

Evolutionary planners are **comfortable with ambiguity** and are willing to take a certain amount of risk to move a plan forward and maintain momentum. Evolutionaries are change agents in the organization, and in order to change, Evolutionaries know the most important thing is to keep the team moving. They understand that they cannot wait for the "perfect" plan – they have to be willing to take action when a plan is "good enough." The most successful planners from vision to execution are those that will move forward with some degree of ambiguity in the plan. Evolutionaries bring transformational change to organizations precisely because they push forward when others are uncertain. It's not about abandoning the value of comprehensive planning, it's about knowing when to say the appropriate attention to the plan has been achieved.

Finally, Evolutionaries **display adaptability.** The minute that you move from a planning to an operational mode the situation is likely to change. The plan has to be adapted to achieve the desired end state. Some of the best planners and operational teams are found in the Navy SEALs. Our friend and colleague, retired Navy SEAL Captain Steve Ahlberg, tells us that SEAL teams plan, plan, and plan come more. They planned until they want to puke. They plan until they've got it all stuffed in their heads, built 3D models, and "what if'd" every scenario. Then, as Captain Ahlberg explains, *"Five minutes into the operation the situation shows up as being completely different, the wheels come off and it's time to adapt the plan."* This is where Evolutionaries become invaluable. They are comfortable with ambiguity, confident in the mission and the team and able to adapt quickly to keep things on track to achieve the desired end state. Evolutionaries are not easily flustered in times of uncertainty, because they anticipate the unexpected and train themselves to respond as a matter of course.

Like Captain Ahlberg, the best Evolutionary leaders bring calm to chaos. Evolutionaries are pros at sharing the planning process and repeating the plan and all of its scenarios over and over until everyone knows it so well it guides team actions unerringly. Ahlberg reminds us that in the SEAL teams *"Everyone knows the plan. Everyone has the same intelligence."* Evolutionaries know that everyone on the team will need to display adaptability when the situation inevitably changes, and the best way to help people adapt to new situations is to make sure everyone on the team knows what is expected. Evolutionary planning is not about holding all the cards and heroically doling out ideas when the time is at hand. Evolutionaries make sure the plan belongs to everyone from the very beginning.

In summary, Evolutionary plans increase your options and your confidence and are clear, inspiring stories for employees to rally around. Evolutionary plans leverage organizational interdependence and cross-departmental synergy by ensuring that strategic objectives are always organizational in nature – not departmental. Finally, Evolutionary plans identify measurable areas of improvement that are directly related to problem solving and the real world tactical challenges faced day-to-day within the organization. It's about moving beyond organizational strategy to a strong value-driven approach to framing the future you want to achieve. Truly Evolutionary plans are magic beans that most organizations throw away or de-value. The organizations that will win in the future are those that realize the huge potential of these short, compelling, public-facing "invitations" to a new way to think and work in the global economy.

CHAPTER 3: EVOLUTIONARY LEADERSHIP

Mountains could be made from books that have been written on the topic of leadership. Some are great, some are terrible, some are based in theory and some focus on more practical experience and application. We have read many of them and believe that you should too. This chapter is not about defining all that is good or necessary when it comes to leading organizations. Instead, we focus on the specific characteristics that distinguish those leaders who consistently and effectively lead transformational change in their organizations from all the other excellent leaders that also exist in business today.

Again, we stress that Evolutionary Leaders are not necessarily the best leaders. Some organizations need to remain stable, weather a storm, or even phase out specific lines of business. New ideas, innovation and transformative change would be foolhardy endeavors. In these cases, the last thing you need is an Evolutionary Leader. But, for those organizations that need to transform, implement big changes, innovate or find new ways to survive and thrive, read on.

First and foremost, Evolutionary Leaders are driven by a passion for what they do. This passion is authentic. There is no "CEO talent search" strategy that will work to find the latest *Forbes* cover executive and offer him or her millions to be your Evolutionary. Evolutionary Leaders are, by definition, emotionally committed to the cause they pursue. Evolutionary Leaders believe in their work, their mission, and their potential. Evolutionary Leaders are definitely authentic. They are comfortable with who they are, and they know why they do what they do. They have committed a piece of themselves to their work – are willing to tie their hearts as well as their minds to the outcomes of their teams and organizations. This deep connection to a sense of purpose allows Evolutionary Leaders to be courageous– a key component of Evolutionary Leadership, as these leaders constantly pioneer new territory and take chances on the unknown.

By understanding why they do what they do, Evolutionary Leaders are liberated to accomplish truly extraordinary things. Part of the secret to accomplishing great things is to proudly exclaim to the public what you are attempting to achieve. Most leaders, even very good leaders, are not comfortable sharing their dreams with the world.

HOW EVOLUTIONARIES LEAD

In his last years, C.K. Prahalad, Professor of Strategy at the University of Michigan Ross School of Business, taught his students that the best leaders "...understand the importance of nonconformity. Leadership is about change, hope, and the future. Leaders have to venture into uncharted territory, so they must be able to handle intellectual solitude and ambiguity." In other words, leaders often feel lonely. Evolutionary Leaders cope well with such loneliness because they know who they are and believe deeply in what they are trying to accomplish. It is such a sense of conviction that allows Evolutionary Leaders to persevere in the face of countless failed ideas, strategies, projects, and prototypes. It's this unique combination of confidence, drive and compassion that enables Evolutionary Leaders to gather followers and get things done.

Evolutionary Leaders:

- *Possess "Street Credibility"*
- *Know who they are*
- *Garner trust, respect and followers*
- *Will make final decisions*

There is no doubt that Evolutionary leaders know their business. Whether they possess a great deal of formal education, lots of on-the-job experience, or a heaping helping of both — one thing is certain, inside of their organizations, Evolutionary leaders *possess "street credibility."* We recognize that the elements that make one credible differ depending on the type of business. For example, in a science lab, having a PhD in Neuroscience might be your calling card for gaining respect. But it would mean very little in a mechanic's shop where they repair cars for a living. So, when we talk about *street credibility* in your business, we simply mean that the people in your organization firmly believe that you know what you are talking about. Are you qualified to lead in your company? Are you able to judge the quality of other kinds of information and communications? We are talking about the premise that your ability to lead people through transformational change is a function of the perceived credibility of your position, your strategies, your presentations, your emails... you get the idea. This may sound like common sense, and it is, but you might be surprised how many leaders we see that are missing this critical component of Evolutionary leadership.

Evolutionary leaders **know who they are**. Sure, you could easily argue that this kind of self-awareness is the subject of a whole other book – or even a religion, maybe! But that is the power of reflected appraisal. Reflected appraisal is the phenomenon of mirroring the judgments of the people around you. And the judgments of the significant others around you have more weight. It is not that your identity is a function of the people around you, it is that your identity is a function of the *significance that you give* to what the people around you say. As you develop your Evolutionary competencies, you are less and less reliant on the opinions of others to compose your own identity and sense of right or wrong, good work or bad work, correct behavior or incorrect behavior. For more in-depth study of this evolutionary development we recommend reading the works of Robert Kegan, PhD, a professor of Psychology at Harvard University. Dr. Kegan describes this progressive growth as moving through "orders of mind." The point is that we are always comparing ourselves to those around us, but each of us is influenced in different ways and to differing degrees by these observations. This is one of those areas where Evolutionary Leaders stand out from other leaders because they are able to act without requiring as much validation from the society around them. In fact they may see too much validation as a sign that they are not "doing their job" as well as they should be. The key thing to remember is that you are in control of with whom you are comparing yourself. How high do you look? Where do you identify your "peers" in leadership?

Evolutionary leaders may not find appropriate comparisons in those nearest to them – sometimes you have to look beyond your social sphere to find leaders that make good comparisons.

Evolutionary leaders are also comfortable with the notion of having more than one leadership "identity" – that there are times when they will step back and hand over authority to someone else on the team. The Evolutionary leader is able to adapt and create a collaborative leadership identity so that everyone in the organization is legitimately participating in the *construction* of the leadership identity, and that is not seen as a threat to the Evolutionary leader. Because at the end of the day, the Evolutionary leader is a construct in much the same way that Generals, with all the badges and insignias of rank, are self-delusional when they think they are fundamentally different than anyone else. They play a role. Sure, not everyone can play that role well, but it is the role that is a function of a social construction that depends on everyone around them to uphold that construction. The day people don't buy-in anymore is the day the illusion is dispelled. And that leads to our next point.

Evolutionary Leaders have mastered the ability to **garner trust, respect and followers.** Any good strategy will have a reliable road map. Taking people off the beaten path to achieve change or innovation is all well and good, but there must still be a path. People follow leaders who know where they are going and are unwavering in their commitment to reach the end state. Evolutionary leaders foster confidence because they know who they are and they have a strong emotional commitment to the vision – this stability in the wake of change and innovation (fundamentally instable forces) is the key to building trust, respect and followers. At the end of the day what people want from a leader is to know two things: do you have a plan and are you going to take me with you?

Finally, momentum is an essential part of the evolutionary experience and that means Evolutionary leaders **will make final decisions** to keep the team moving ahead at all times. Evolutionary leaders make judgment calls and people rely on them to be experienced and intelligent in making tough decisions. Teams are really looking for action, teams are really looking for something to do, so at some point, every good leader has to be comfortable with stopping a conversation and saying *"Okay, I have heard what all of you have to say, now here is what we are going to do. This is the next step, and this is the step after that."* Evolutionary leaders understand that successful leadership depends on reliability, and that sort of credibility, once earned, is not guaranteed forever. You have to constantly replenish the account by making decisions and continuously moving forward.

CHAPTER 4: EVOLUTIONARY COMMUNICATION

Communication is the key to establishing our competencies and talents and to demonstrating our sincerity. Evolutionary Communicators know the value of authentic communication when it comes to driving transformational change. Authenticity is a term that has been overused in the past few years when talking about everything from leadership to branding to sales. What we mean by authenticity is that Evolutionary Communicators place their *motive* at the center of their communication efforts. The presence of human motive is the root of action – it's what motivates ourselves and those around us to commit to a course and achieve results. When Evolutionary Communicators place motive at the center of their communication efforts, they achieve clarity. Others are better able to understand the Evolutionary Communicator's driving values and purpose for acting. This communication behavior is exactly what people are referring to when they talk about someone's "integrity." Whether you call it authenticity, honesty, being straight-forward, or just a "straight-shooter" – motive-led communication is at the heart of transformative change.

An Evolutionary Communicator is like a master of communication aikido. Aikido is a martial art form based in the belief that you can defend yourself by effectively using the energy and momentum of your opponent rather than generating new energy. Most leaders we meet tell us that communication in their organizations is really tough – that it takes a ton of energy and time. So, inevitably people slack off on good communication practices because they feel that doing it well is just too hard. It's like constantly swimming upstream. But we believe that even when you *stop* communicating, you are saying something. If you buy the premise that you cannot opt out of communicating (even not communicating will be interpreted by others as having some sort of meaning), then it is actually impossible to not communicate. So if you can't not communicate, then the question is: what are you communicating? Where Evolutionary Communicators stand out is that they can use the current mechanisms and traditions of the organization's communication culture to introduce or reinforce key strategic messages – especially messages around change and transformation. In other words, they are experts at adapting their communication to their audience.

It is essential in any organization that negative feedback flow easily so that problems and choke points in a plan can be addressed quickly. The Evolutionary Communicator is the organic, informal message sender that can name and recognize the reality of what is happening in the field and generate an effective feedback loop to top leadership that is mission-critical for any strategy's success. When you have Evolutionary Communicators monitoring and driving your strategic messaging, your organization can achieve transformative change faster and with more lasting success as new ways of exchanging, sharing and funneling information become ingrained in the very nature of how work gets done.

How Evolutionaries Communicate

Research conducted by Sandy Pentland of MIT's Human Dynamics Lab, published in the *Harvard Business Review* in January 2010, shows that the more successful people are more energetic communicators – that "It's not what you say, it's how you say it." The study used established science to predict with an 87% degree of accuracy which executives would win a business competition or sales pitch solely on the basis of the social signals they send. Devices that recorded data on their social signals – tone of voice, gesticulation, proximity to others and more – predicted each winner without reading or hearing the actual pitches." (Note: judges that only read the pitches chose different winners.)

The winning executives talked more than those that were not so successful. But the study showed the key difference between the winners and the losers was that the winning executives also *listened* more. By talking more – sharing their stories and asking lots of questions – they were better able to elicit responses from others. And when people responded, they listened closely. From these conversations they gathered feedback, learned preferences, and spent time really getting to know people. They put a lot of themselves out there, and they got a lot in return. Perhaps the most interesting outcome of the study was the discovery that the more of these sorts of people that were placed together on a team the better that team performed.

Evolutionary Communicators are a lot like the executives in the study described above. They understand that communication is not just about transferring information – but about building relationships and garnering support to achieve positive outcomes. We see Evolutionary communication as the need to express influence, and to be an agent of leadership and change in the organization. It is about making great presentations, managing meetings effectively, writing great e-mails and positively participating in the hundreds of informal conversations that take place each week. It is an expression of action and deliberation. Philosopher Kenneth Burke would call this an "impulse to action."

Evolutionary Communicators:
- *Are inclusive*
- *Constantly refine*
- *Are effective*
- *Use media-centered strategies*

The Evolutionary Communicator is *inclusive,* using a broad palate of resources and voices, a wide array of research and data, and a lot of people. Evolutionary Communicators are comfortable getting a lot of "fingerprints" on a project and broadening the dialogue early in the process. Yes, that does mean projects can take longer. But the results will become a more lasting and effective component of the organization's culture. Evolutionaries know that when you build people into the processes and the strategy, you have a stronger foundation from which you can grow, innovate and lead as an organization.

Evolutionary Communicators take responsibility for "netting" out major points and *refining* themes from the conversations they are in. They see it as their job. They can quickly and easily take the 20 pages of dialogue and create one slide that synthesizes and refines the salient issues. And they know how to use this talent to gather buy-in, rally the troops and get things done. They become the "go to" leaders in their organizations because they have the valuable information people need and are willing to share what they know in ways that teach others and build community. Refining, at its core, is about creating clarity. And Evolutionary Communicators know that clarity is what teams need to stay motivated, keep momentum, and reach a desirable end state. One of the most effective ways to achieve clarity and gain influence with others is to use the power of narrative – to tell a good story. In his book, *Simplicity*, Bill Jensen explains that if you want to create clarity you have to look for something that defines a common meaning for everyone. Evolutionary Communicators know that "something" is storytelling. They are masters at

- Moving beyond the data to tell the larger, value-based story
- Connecting that goal at hand to the larger strategic vision
- Using great metaphors or every-day comparisons to explain the "heart" of an idea
- Using the story to cut through the noise of everyday business to quickly make the complex clear

And perhaps most importantly, the Evolutionary Communicator knows how to give that message back to the ecosystem from which it came. They don't claim ownership of the dialogue or its outcomes, but see themselves as a facilitator and refiner of the conversation that already belongs to the community of stakeholders involved. Easily communicating without needing to have the power or control over the communication is what makes Evolutionaries so *effective*. Evolutionary Communicators excel by learning the language of the culture they are working in. Their ability to become fluent in the language of the team, organization or community allow them to quickly build credibility, demonstrate understanding of challenges and opportunities, and sell their ideas.

The Evolutionary Communicator is completely aware that in the best case scenario the message is going out as widely as possible and that means using a *media-centered* approach to communicating. They use these messages to create buy-in and to effectively spread the word. They always err on the side of more transparency. They are not afraid of sharing and over-sharing. Evolutionary Communicators are not good corporate secret-keepers! They are going to be thinking of building walking decks and short videos and interview pieces to share the vision, educate people and garner followers through a narrative that people can rally around. They use messages to create alignment. They use media to be even more inclusive, to actively empower more people to join the conversation – thus the media acts as an invitation to the conversation. But the media is also critical because it helps to ensure the consistency of the conversation; it controls the message so that everyone in the conversation is using the same language to engage in the dialogue.

- *Note: it is a given assumption that the media has a short shelf-life. This is not about high-end marketing pieces, but the day-to-day methods of utilizing in-house resources to create media "on the go" that can be used in real time.*

You will recall that one of the lessons offered early in this chapter is that Evolutionary Communicators know how to adapt their message and style to their audience to make an impact. The best way to adapt to your audience is to have a solid understanding of how you communicate naturally, and how your audience prefers to communicate. In other words, you need to know about Communication Orientations.

Communication Orientation

A significant amount of research in the area of Social Cognition confirms the idea that people see the characteristics of "successful" communication very differently. For example, some people see conflict as a sign of trouble. Others see conflict as a natural and expected part of social interaction – it is normal, even healthy. If you learn about these characteristics, you will understand yourself better and you will be able to better understand the point of view (or "orientation") that others bring to their communications. Researchers use three different categories to describe our basic communication orientation:

Direct
- Direct communicators **say what they think** – and they don't necessarily think about how others will receive

the message. They don't mind conflict and see conflict as a natural part of communicating.

- Direct communicators don't view communication as being all that complicated. They believe that they have communicated effectively when they have a thought, and they say it.
- Direct communicators are consistent in their approach. They don't change their behaviors much from one situation to the next.
- Direct communicators may not attend to all the rules of polite conversation. And they do not necessarily value all of those rules when others speak to them.

Situational
- Situational communicators believe that we will all get along a lot better if we all **know our roles**, and **follow the rules**.
- Situational communicators believe that they have communicated effectively when they say or do the right thing for the specific situation. These people align their communication with conventional roles and strive to say what is "appropriate" in a given situation.
- Situational communicators tend to be very concerned about how other people feel, and they see conflict as a problem.
- Situational communicators like to know all of the expectations that are present in a given situation so that they can be prepared and appropriate.

Bonding

- Bonding communicators are interested in whatever the **other person** is interested in. This is not an insincere interest. They will talk about mountain climbing for an hour with someone who is interested in mountain climbing – even though they have shown no interest in it themselves in the past.

- Bonding communicators believe they have communicated successfully when they have created a bond with the person with whom they are speaking.

- Bonding communicators tend to downplay formal rules and roles if it will help build a better bond. They might say, for example, "Don't think of me as your manager..." in order to elevate the person-to-person relationship.

- Bonding communicators adapt to every person they speak with, so their communication style will change a lot – even in a single situation.

Know Your Communication Orientation

Self-awareness with regard to how we craft our messages is an essential step in enhancing our communication so that others can actually hear us more clearly. What's more, when we know our own tendencies we can better comprehend and contend with the tendencies of those around us so that we, in turn, can hear them without our own defensive reactions getting in the way.

So get out your Number Two pencils and prepare to take a quick quiz. Answer honestly – reflecting not the way you'd *like* to be, or the way you're trying to be, but the way you are. Remember, there is no "best" way to be and no organization could survive without people who fall into all three categories: Bonding, Situational and Direct.

QUIZ

Please circle the number (5–1) that best corresponds to your thinking about each of the fifteen statements listed below:

5 – STRONGLY AGREE **4** – AGREE **3** – NEUTRAL **2** – DISAGREE **1** – STRONGLY DISAGREE

1.	I am a "get to the point" kind of person.	5	4	3	2	1
2.	I like to know the details about what is expected in work situations.	5	4	3	2	1
3.	If I am in a good conversation, I can stay focused even in a noisy or busy atmosphere.	5	4	3	2	1
4.	People describe me as being very consistent.	5	4	3	2	1
5.	I work best when I know what role I am supposed to play and the roles that others are supposed to play.	5	4	3	2	1
6.	I don't have to actually be personally involved in something to be interested in	5	4	3	2	1

	it; I like to hear about mountain climbing – even though I am not a climber myself.					
7.	It is best to be direct when you are offering criticism or bad news.	5	4	3	2	1
8.	I try to respect other people's points of view when I am in conversation with them even if I don't agree.	5	4	3	2	1
9.	It is very satisfying to meet people and develop a genuine connection with them.	5	4	3	2	1
10.	Conflict is a natural part of communication; you just have to deal with it as best you can.	5	4	3	2	1
11.	Communication is based on reciprocity, give and take, working together.	5	4	3	2	1
12.	People describe me as being very adaptive; I make friends quickly.	5	4	3	2	1
13.	In general there is too much chitchat and pointless conversation in the workplace.	5	4	3	2	1
14.	The best managers set out very clear expectations and organizational rules.	5	4	3	2	1
15.	The key to communication is personal empathy and being	5	4	3	2	1

able to connect with the other person's point of view.

Scoring the Quiz

The statements on this quiz speak to a series of different approaches to business communication. The key statements focus on a series of communication styles defined as:

- *Direct*
- *Situational*
- *Bonding*

To score your quiz:

- Calculate your total for items 1, 4, 7, 10, and 13. This is your Direct Score.
- Calculate your total for items 2, 5, 8, 11, and 15. This is your Situational Score.
- Calculate your total for items 3, 6, 9, 12, and 14. This is your Bonding Score.

Interpreting Your Results

These communication orientations are based in part on a significant body of research in communication theory begun by Dr. Jesse Delia at the University of Illinois. The nice thing about this work is that it does not seem to be dependent on gender, socioeconomic status, or education; the theory gets at the "basic" assumptions that shape our approach to communication.

If you have a high Direct score, then you are most likely very comfortable with your approach to communication and you are probably wondering what all of the fuss is about.

If you have a high Situational score, then you are probably attuned to situational cues. You are probably very perceptive and sensitive to the dynamics from one situation to the next. You appreciate clarity in communication and roles. You work hard to make sure that feelings are not hurt.

If you have a high Bonding score, you are probably what others would call a "people person." You value making connection with others. You have a wide range of interests and you see great conversation as an end in and of itself.

If you have several high scores, you are probably Bonding with a "preferred" approach that is Situational or Direct. The theory suggests that Bonding speakers have the capacity to access any of the styles, and that Situational speakers can access the Direct style – though they probably feel uncomfortable if they are forced to be Direct. Direct speakers are happy being just the way they are. Use these scores as general indicators of your stylistic preferences.

Please read on to learn more about your communication orientation in terms of its strong points and potential pitfalls. But – and this is crucial – be sure to read about the other two categories as well if you are interested in being able to communicate clearly to everyone in every situation.

Direct Speakers

What's So Great About Direct Speakers?
There are many advantages to being a Direct speaker. Everyone knows where they stand with you, and even if they don't like where they stand, this is actually a quite valuable thing to know. Unlike those bonding chameleons, you are also extremely consistent in what you say and how you say it. Everyone is well aware of who will show up and

what they will "get" when they invite you to their meeting or their party.

You keep your remarks brief and to the point. Your communication is uncomplicated (no, not dumbed down, just uncomplicated). The simplicity of your discourse can offer a breath of fresh air in a world where so many others speak in jargon, euphemism, bet-hedging equivocation or hyper cautious legalese. You call it like you see it, and often you are the one to say what no one else around you will dare to. In the classic fairy tale, you would have been the boy who shouted out "The emperor has no clothes!"

Most admirable of all, you are an authentic individual, true to yourself and to what you believe. Artifice and pretense are not for you. Even people who are put off by your style of communication will never call you hypocritical or two-faced.

But here's the bad news; they are going to call you some other things.

How Direct Speakers Make Others Crazy

Undiplomatic, brusque, rude, oblivious to the feelings of others, shallow and uncompassionate: does this sound like anyone you know? Chances are that as a Direct speaker you do not see yourself this way. As far as you are concerned you are being honest and straightforward. It's true you do not go out of your way to spare anyone's feelings, but at least you're not wasting anyone's time.

The problem is that in spite of your many strengths, there are people who cannot absorb what you say because they are suspect of your motives. Some think you cannot control your impulses. They fear that you are dangerous, a loose cannon who might go off on them at any second. Some just think you are mean.

That said, one of the conundrums about being a Direct speaker is that some of you can get away with it more than others can. If you're, say, a brain surgeon or an airline pilot – a specially skilled professional on whom others' lives may literally depend – you're pretty much allowed to say whatever you want with impunity. In fact, doing so adds to your cachet. If you're an ultra-successful maverick entrepreneur or infallible investment guru, or self-made billionaire in any field, you're never perceived as rude, just colorful. But if you're more of an average mortal, even a very talented one, it would benefit you immeasurably to try to bridge any interpersonal communication gaps you could be suffering.

Direct types generally make outstanding leaders, especially for high-paced organizations. We have found in our experience that many Evolutionaries we have met are Direct communicators. Their approach enables them to cut through the clutter, focus on what's most important, and translate their values into action. But your leadership will be most effective when you step outside of your stream of consciousness for a bit and notice what is going on around you.

Clarifying Strategies for Direct Speakers

For Direct speakers – as well as the other two types of communicators – the most important thing is to simply acknowledge that other worldviews exist and are valid. All the orientations work in different ways, but all must work in concert.

But it's not enough to simply think, "Okay, I know you other folks are out there." As a Direct speaker, the onus falls on you to make certain that your directness is not misinterpreted. Yes, you want your words to be taken at face value, but such is not human nature. Like it or not, others draw inferences from what you say. The quality of their inferential process in detecting and ascribing motive allows them to interpret a critical comment as a personal offense or as a key piece of coaching.

We know what you're thinking: What am I, a mind reader? No, you're not. That's why you need to ask questions. If you've just evaluated someone's work in your usual no-holds barred manner, remember that he or she might not have taken it in the objective spirit in which you genuinely offered it. Ask: Are you okay? Did I upset you? Do you understand why I said what I did and why I need you to do what I asked?

We are not suggesting that you back off from who you are – only that you remember to check in after a conversation. And even more critical – be clear about your motive for your communication right from the beginning. Say, *"I am sharing this feedback with you because I believe you have great potential in your work, and I feel you have what it takes to use the feedback I am giving you to achieve excellence.*" It might sound like "a pain" to have to be more explicit about your motive for giving feedback, but that is not a good excuse for not doing it. Participating in a culture involves a continual trade-off of costs and rewards. It will cost you some time and effort to do the additional communication work, but your reward will be that others will be far more able to take in what you say and act on it in a positive way rather than nurse hurts and grievances that will stand not only in their way but also in yours.

Situational Speakers

What's So Great About Situational Speakers?

We have already mentioned that the three communication orientations exist along a continuum. Picture Direct types at the far left and Bonders at the far right. Situational types are in the middle.

Now picture that each type has a set of building blocks. These blocks form their worldview; from them each type tries to build structures to accommodate every communication situation. As a Situational type you start out with more blocks to work with than do Direct types. You can create more configurations, and so you have more options and more flexibility.

You are good at and dedicated to manifesting just the right "face" at just the right time once you have defined any given situation. At a meeting you'll wear your no-nonsense meeting face; at the after-work bowling alley party you'll wear your affable bowling face (and your bowling shoes because you always know what the rules are and like to follow them).

You rely on and value blocks of structured time that connote a certain social meaning. At work, you are the one that makes sure the Monday morning meeting happens and that everyone has an agenda; at home you are the one who champions the family dinner hour, plans get-togethers with the neighbors and relatives and never forgets a birthday or anniversary.

You are just as organized about thoughts as you are about time – good at framing things and placing them in conceptual buckets so that you and others can make sense of them. Your knack for remembering things has often gotten others out of a jam. (When planning for a camping trip, you're the one who remembers to pack the tent stakes, the flashlight batteries and the compass.)

In short, you are great at "care and feeding." You are a stabilizing force, the glue stick of your workplace. No organization could thrive, or even survive, without you. We have found that fewer Evolutionaries have a Situational communication orientation. It is less suited to the transformational change they so often seek in their careers and their lives.

How Situationals Can Make Others Crazy

Sometimes life is not fair. Sometimes things do not fit into neat categories. And sometimes you have to do things that fall outside of the realm of your official job description in order to accomplish a goal, change an organization or solve a problem. All of this disturbs Situational communicators, and when you are disturbed you dig in your heels about enforcing the rules and roles you hold so dear.

But to Direct types, who just want to move forward, rules or no, and to Bonders, who live to cross even the most well-established boundaries, you are a buzz killer – a card-carrying member of the fun police. As much as these other types may value your skills and reliability when things are running along normally, they will cite you for "driving them to distraction" in any situation that they feel calls for fast change and ad hoc solutions. Let's face it: you are generally not at your best when things are in flux. Rapid change offends your innate sense of order and your affinity for tradition.

Another complaint that is sometimes heard about Situationals is that you are superficial. Your responses can be so situation-driven that Bonders suspect you give the human element short shrift. Although you are the kind of person who can have a heartfelt cry at a stranger's funeral – so caught up are you in the situation and its attendant expectations – others may see such behavior as indicative less of empathy than of rote conformity.

Clarifying Strategies for Situationals
As a Situational, what you do is valuable and important. One of the things you need to do more of is to let people know that – and to remember that yourself. Don't get so caught up in your tasks that you neglect to notice that without you and others like you, your

organization would be far more chaotic and inefficient. Your motive is to keep the social structure in place, and you are good at it.

On the other hand, it wouldn't hurt you to lighten up a little bit. Yes, meetings have to happen but they don't have to be as painful as they usually are. Think about helping your colleagues to have better meetings – perhaps ones that allow for a little off-the-agenda banter and brainstorming, or perhaps even ones that take place at the bowling alley between frames.

We are not asking you to morph into another type of person. But you can be more cognizant of others' motives and try not to take things so personally. Sure, being in the middle of the communication spectrum, you still get some abuse from both sides, but don't let it throw you. Be philosophical about it: "Ah, here comes the abuse, it's right on time." Deep down, remain calm in the knowledge of how much everyone needs you.

Bonding Speakers

What's So Great about Bonding Speakers?

Boy, are you fun to go out to lunch with and to travel with! You are someone who makes friends wherever you go, not to mention your ability to get the bartender to pour you and all your colleagues free shots of tequila whenever you're in the mood.

Charismatic and charming, you are able to find something in common with virtually everyone and begin to forge a relationship based on that commonality. What's more, you believe that business is all about the relationship.

Of all the types, you also have the biggest number of building blocks in your block box. You can structure your communication so that it mirrors the communication of anyone with whom you are trying to make a connection. At the extreme of this orientation, Bonders can identify equally with almost anyone. They like snowboarding; you like snowboarding — or else you would like to like snowboarding and hope they will enlighten you about its many joys along with the particulars of where to do it, when to do it, how to do it and what equipment you will need.

Anything but an elitist, you are an equal opportunity connection-maker. To you, everyone is interesting and anyone is as interesting as the next person. If you've ever watched the show *Dirty Jobs* on the Discovery Channel, you'll spy this trait in the show's host, Mike Rowe. Rowe celebrates unsung heroes who do unthinkable jobs that few of us would want to take on. He profiles everyone from sludge recyclers, hippo keepers and bug breeders, to salt miners, pig farmers and pigeon poop cleaner-uppers. Not afraid to get his own hands dirty in the process, Rowe is genuinely fascinated with each and every job he surveys, and he sincerely values each person who does each job.

As a Bonder, you have time for everyone, or at least you have the heartfelt desire to make time. And when you do spend time with someone you leave them with the impression that at that moment they are the most important person you have ever encountered. This can be highly motivational for those that interact with a Bonding communicator. Many Evolutionaries we have worked with possess this Bonding trait. They know how to connect quickly, establish meaningful relationships as a matter of course, and inspire people to believe not only in an idea, but in their ability to do almost anything!

All in all, you sound like a pretty great human being. So: why on earth do so many people get angry with you so often?

For one thing, people can see Bonders as fickle. Sure, they might feel good when they are on the Bonder's radar screen, but they feel betrayed when the Bonder has moved on to bonding with someone else.

Bonders are often pegged with being indecisive as well – or conversely, incredibly decisive as you frequently make snap decisions in the spur of the moment. Because Bonders can find a way to agree with almost everyone, many people come away thinking that they've convinced you that their idea or approach to a given situation is best. But if they listen carefully, they will hear that Bonders are not given to firm commitment. You couch your agreements in what some call weasel-speak: _I think we might be able to...; I think it's important to reach out...; It would be super if we could do that._ Too often all this _faux_ agreement just confuses the issue at hand and incites conflict instead of resolving it.

Bonders are also accused of being so busy bonding that you forget you are accountable for deliverables. And it is true that at times Bonders can be more interested in the conversation than the end game. There are a few people in the world whose entire job is solely about bonding. In your dream scenario, Bonders would only have to do lunch – that's it – and it is understood that others will follow through with the details. But most of us in the real world do not enjoy that luxury.

For obvious reasons, we are not suggesting that Bonders surrender their many charms. Your ability to captivate and inspire those around you gives you incredible Evolutionary potential. However, it is important to focus on the end game – outcomes are paramount. Periodically ask: "What am I producing?" and "What is the goal?"

We mentioned before that Bonders have more communication building blocks than any other type. They are a bit like those Eskimos that have 16 words for snow, or like oenophiles who have 183 ways to describe the taste of a wine. But just because you have a lot of blocks does not mean it's a good idea to play with all of the blocks all of the time. Fortunately, you can always downsize to a subset, taking your cues from the Situational or Direct orientation. You do not need to abandon who you are, but keep in mind that there is no shame – and sometimes a lot of merit – in saying to someone, for example, "I love you like a brother, but we have to get this work done."

Before you go too far down the bonding road, check in with yourself and see if you're about to overstep your bounds. If so, consider this piece of Will Rogers' advice*: Never miss a good opportunity to shut up.*

LAY YOUR MOTIVES ON THE TABLE

Now we have been around long enough to know that no matter what communication orientation you fall into, you are not going to instantly take all of our advice — no matter how much you paid for this book. It takes time and practice to "step outside yourself," broaden your range and alter long-entrenched habits. So, while you are working on traversing your own Evolutionary path, we will reinforce just one essential communication lesson to hold onto: When you feel that someone is misunderstanding you or that they are feeling threatened by what you are saying, lay your motive on the table. Whether your motive *is I want to crush the competition* or *I want to beat this deadline* or *I want to follow the rules* or *I want to stop following the rules and have some fun for a change*, just say so. You would be amazed how many problems this will eliminate before they can take root.

Remember, communication is multi-layered:

- There is you and there is me.
- There is your perception of me.
- And then there is my perception of your perception of me.

These three levels drive functional and dysfunctional relationships. If you've been married or in a significant romantic relationship for, say, more than an hour you know how this works. You and your loved one are having a chat. You say something — *innocently enough* — about guessing there's not much food in fridge. They scowl and fold their arms across their chest. They hear you accusing them of not shopping for dinner. You were about to ask them out to dinner but now they seem like they are in such a bad mood for *no reason* that you have second thoughts. You both eat leftovers in silence and go to bed angry.

R.D. Laing called this "the spiral of reciprocating perspectives." At your house you might call it Thursday. But you know what we mean. Think how much grief you could have saved if you'd said, *"I'm starved. Want to go to Red Lobster?"*

It's not our goal to make psychotherapists of everyone. This is not mumbo-jumbo. Just say what you want and — here's the really important part — *say why you want it*. What are the reasons behind your stated goal? How did you arrive at this decision or preference? Did you reject any other options? What will the decision's impact be? The more clarity you can bring to your motive in every situation the better off everyone is. Evolutionary Communicators are masters of laying their motives on the table. And that's essential for lasting and successful transformational change initiatives.

People evaluate your communication as successful to the extent that they feel they have visibility into your motives and they resonate with those motives. A 2006 study that surveyed roughly 300 managers and employees at over 100 U.S. employers found that employees of companies where decisions were explained more fully were more than twice as likely to support those decisions as workers who got less information. And needless to say, support translates into effort, enthusiasm and accomplishment. Conversely, when people don't know why a new initiative has come down from on high they are apt to resist it. They're not being deliberately uncooperative. They just have nothing to hold onto.

CHAPTER 5: EVOLUTIONARY TEAMS

All you have to do is tune into national news to know that the Navy SEALs train awesome teams. The SEAL teams do the impossible, make "miracles" happen, defy all odds. With a single mission, they can change the world. In short, they are the model for what it means to be truly Evolutionary. Like many curious observers before us, we asked Captain Steve Ahlberg, "How do you create Evolutionary Teams?"

CAPTAIN STEVE AHLBERG: In Basic Underwater Demolition/SEAL (BUD/S) training, we call the exercises we put people through "evolutions" because we believe each step of the training process is an evolutionary process. The evolutions we use work to build what I believe are the best examples of what a Team really is. We train people at every level: individual, pair, small group and entire class. For example, in BUD/S you are tested on an individual level when they tie your hands behind your back, tie your feet together, and throw you in the swimming pool. You are expected to swim several lengths of the pool, go to the bottom in the deep end and pick up a diving mask in your mouth and then continue to bob up and down or tread water until an instructor tells you to get out. At first when the instructors tell you about the evolution you think, "Oh this is going to be really hard, I may not be able to do it, I might have to quit." But then you find out that you can do it – most people in the training can do it – and you learn a lot about yourself and what makes you tick and what motivates you. You are also paired with a swim buddy and conduct various evolutions as a pair, such as long swims in the ocean. We put people in pairs to see if they can work with one other person – that is the key to teams – if you can work well with one other person, then you can likely work well in a team. For the longest of our swims, the top half of the class (the first pairs to finish the swim) got hot showers, but for the second half of the class, the hot water would not be available so you got a cold shower. It always "paid to be a winner"! Additionally, it wasn't just a straight swim because there was a huge seaweed bed in the center. The instructors warn you not to try taking a shortcut across it, but people still try and they inevitably get tangled and slowed in the process. The best route is to swim the long way around. You have to stay disciplined as a pair and not try what appears from your perspective in the water to be a shortcut. You want to finish as quickly as possible but you don't want to swim too fast and stress your swim buddy out nor do you want your buddy to swim too fast and feel like you are holding him back. You want to swim together, swim in harmony, and communicate to determine your strategy for the entire swim. This teaches you to really communicate with someone else, how to motivate each other, and finish successfully. In groups of seven people (a boat crew), you are given a small rubber boat to take everywhere with you. You paddle it for miles and you carry it on your heads for miles. The instructors have you paddle out through the surf, flip the boats over, then flip them back, get back in, land it and launch it on boulders, and use the boat as a place to elevate your feet as you do push ups. Every time you do an evolution with the boat incorrectly you have to do it again. The trick is to learn how to stay motivated, work together, and keep communicating effectively and clearly. You start out using a lot of four-letter words! But soon you learn there are better and more meaningful ways to communicate to get the job done. It's in these type of evolutions that you learn how to be a leader, how to communicate, how to plan, how to strategize, how to problem solve, and how to engage in teamwork. As a whole class you go on long runs – up to 16 miles – in formation on the beach in boots and long pants. The goal is to both meet the required time and to stick together as a class. Of course you have people with different levels of running ability so getting the whole class through the run together in formation is a matter of planning, teamwork, communication, strategy, and motivation. You have a team goal to start as a group and end as a group. If you don't finish as a class, you do it all over again. This is where you learn how to help others, how to ask for help when you need it, and how to be receptive to help when it is offered. Before I got to BUD/S, I had taken classes on team building and leadership but nothing was ever this effective.

If you are anything like us, you are probably pretty impressed by that story. But you might also be thinking, "Sure, elite teams like the Navy SEALs can operate like that, but what about us mere mortals trying to wrestle with Excel reports and timesheets? How does this work in business?" We asked that same question, and here's what Captain Ahlberg had to say.

CAPTAIN STEVE AHLBERG: I have seen experiential training work with banks, construction companies, youth groups, in many places of business. People think they might be the best leader in the world and/or on the organizational chart they are the leader, but in experiential situations they may find that no one is following them. It is usually true back at the office as well. During experiential training you learn a lot about yourself and others. My biggest issue concerning Teams in the business world is that they throw a group of people together and call them a team. Real teams are much more than just a group of people. Real teams are groups of people that have complementary skills, are bonded by shared experiences, and have the common vision of a desired end state—they have a reason for being.

Evolutionary Teams are more likely to execute on the organization's strategic objectives because they demand clarity of mission and the sense that it's important. The Evolutionary Team ideally exists with one foot in the traditional "business-as-usual" culture of the organization and one foot in the world of innovation, change and new possibilities. These teams should also enjoy a Charter that completely frees them to be innovative outside of the "business as usual" if your company is ready to take that leap. Evolutionary Teams are truly at their best when the organization is in crisis mode and true revolutionary action is critical for survival. But we find that most organizations are looking for change that is a little less dramatic. And that sort of smaller, but significant strategic shift in an organization is also where Evolutionary Teams excel. Whatever the change on the horizon, what makes Evolutionary Teams special is their transformative potential. Because they have the ability to balance between organizational traditions and pioneering vision, Evolutionary Teams can do what other teams can't: they can raise the bar for what is possible in your organization, your industry, and even the world.

You need Evolutionary Team members because even if the team fails, you will know more and be better off than working with non-Evolutionary Team members. With ordinary team members, giving up is an option. Failing because of team dynamics is an option. Failing because ideas were not vetted well is an option. The team may fail, and you won't necessarily know why. But when you have Evolutionary Team members, even in failure you will have an understanding of how and why that failure happened – and this knowledge will give you confidence in the endeavor. Even if you lose the game, you are assured to know much more about the opponent than you did before.

Pitfalls. The downside to Evolutionary Team members is that they do need to be reined in sometimes. Working with an Evolutionary can sometimes feel as one client of ours says, *"Like trying to boil the ocean."* At some point Evolutionaries will push too far, think too big – it is in their nature to pursue excellence and shoot for the moon. This will not always be practical. But it will be a force that pushes your teams harder and creates the kind of culture where winning as a team is more likely.

HOW EVOLUTIONARIES WORK IN TEAMS

Let's get one thing straight – Evolutionaries *love* to be on teams! Sure, Evolutionaries like "rah rah" and relational development, and that kind of bond is essential for truly high-performing teams. But the driving motivation is to get things done, facilitate meaningful change, and bring about desired results through the work of the team. Evolutionary Teams are inherently outcome oriented. They are willing to engage in efforts that are research-based, process-based or relational-based depending on what is necessary to forward a desired outcome. They will not be happy with "fluffy" interactions for the sake of it. But they will be the first to suggest soft skills training if that's what it takes to better bond the team, to increase morale, and to get the job done.

This also means that the Evolutionary is constantly thinking of the competencies they need to develop to be better members of their teams. That might be learning how to operate a complex piece of machinery or software program. Or it might be to be learning how to order Chinese food in Beijing on the next team business trip. The point is that gaining "badges" in the skills that forward the team toward its goals is seen as a worthy pursuit.

Evolutionary Team Members:

- *Align to the mission of the team*
- *Take pride in being a team member*
- *Have humility around weaknesses*
- *Are supremely confident in their strengths*

Evolutionaries cannot participate where they are not **aligned to the mission of the team.** In just a moment we're going to tell you that humility is an essential Evolutionary characteristic. But for now, we are going to make the observation that a project team's Charter should be audacious – seemingly outrageous. There should be a level of pressure, urgency, importance, criticality, difficulty, that all add up to the inescapable conclusion that there is no way that any individual alone can solve the problem or accomplish the goal and there is no way the organization could solve the problem or accomplish the goal in its normal working patterns. If you create a team to do something that is fundamentally easy or inconsequential or achievable through the normal workings of the organization, then you have woefully damaged the individuals and you have weakened your organization. It is not neutral – from the Evolutionary's point of view, it is much worse to have a team doing something that is not incredibly cool than to do nothing at all. So, the ability to establish your Evolutionary Team on a "burning platform" will do two things: 1) provide the team the focus they need to accomplish an extraordinary goal, and 2) not make that platform part of your ongoing organization. The bottom line here is that you *must make the project important.* If Evolutionary Team members don't feel there is a strong shared value, they will make one up. They simply function from a place where working for something bigger than themselves is always a critical motivator.

Evolutionaries believe that to be a good team player is one of the best characteristics that any human can have. For this reason alone, the Evolutionary **is proud of his or her identity as a team member.** Being a good team member is a personal value for the Evolutionary that is *independent* of any organizational goal or project outcome. This Evolutionary characteristic connects back to our discussion of social identity in leadership. If you can imagine sliding down a fire pole, throwing your gear on, hopping in the truck and then finding yourself in an intense battle against a raging fire, knowing you have to depend on the people around you for your life, then of course you are going to take deep pride in wearing the badge of your team. The emotional trappings of the team become paramount in the way you define who you are. The mistake people tend to make is to say: "Well, let's get our team some shirts." But the magic is not in the shirt, it is in *fighting the fire together*. It is the pride that comes from participating in something bigger than any one person. Evolutionaries understand that shared excellence and failure are how you foster strong team loyalty.

Evolutionary team members **have a sense of humility around their weaknesses.** They are thrilled to be dependent on the talents of other team members in order to accomplish a mission (think of great sports teams). This is not about saying: "Well, Bob is a better numbers person so he should do this task." It's about interlocking strength with support to achieve team end goals. A common mistake people make is to simply divide tasks on a team up by individual skill sets. But what they should be doing is looking for what they can do together by *combining* different skill sets and leveraging the bonding power inherent in partnerships. It is subtle, but important – it's not about stepping back out of humility, but about stepping in and engaging in a way that puts you second to the higher goals of the partner you are bound to and the team. Remember the lesson we learn from the Navy SEALs about the power of working in pairs. Evolutionary team members are going to work exponentially better with a "swim buddy." There is also humility in the learning process associated with recognizing and improving on managing weaknesses as well. If you have to stand on the sidelines for a time to just observe what is happening, then you are still responsible for being an active member of the debrief to share your observations, ideas and opinions. Your point of view is always valuable. You are always a member of the team, whether your skill set is being featured or not.

Evolutionaries are also **supremely confident in their strengths and what they bring to the team.** And this is about bringing the whole game of the team up – bringing these skills to the team raises the bar of the whole team as a collective force. But this is not about being a hero. Evolutionary teams often produce heroes (like SEAL missions) but achieving hero status is not what drives the team. So, just because you are great at designing PowerPoint slides, you should not end up doing the whole project. You have the responsibility to find ways to connect with the opportunities for support, feedback and point of view that come from the other members of the team. And if you know something best and you are not teaching others, then the only conceivable excuse for that from an Evolutionary point of view is that it is not the right time to teach. If you are doing an emergency landing on an airplane, and you are the only one who can land it, it is not a good time to do a seminar on how to land an airplane. But it is your obligation to find a way to teach that skill to others once that plane is landed. That is what it means to be an Evolutionary Team member.

Forming an Evolutionary Team

The secret recipe:

- **Step 1:** Prepare the culture for teamwork. You do this by making short-term, highly manageable assignments to pairs of people. Just as Captain Ahlberg tells us that "if you can't work with one other person, you can't work with a team," you first have to socialize your people to sharing work and sharing accountability. This does not come naturally to most people! Captain Ahlberg tells us that it is three-part cycle, there's the planning piece, then there is the operation and then there is the debrief piece, to create the complete ecosystem for any kind of shared work. You need to teach this to your teams, and hold them accountable to it. This philosophy has to become a part of how all work gets done in the organization. People always ask us for examples. Here's an example:

    > You are looking into adding social media as a part of a new networking piece. You assign two people to this task — one from marketing and one from IT to write a short three- to five-page brief on the classic mistakes that other businesses have made in using social media. They are asked to present their findings in writing and to present them in person at the next management team meeting. Their performance is evaluated in a follow-up meeting with open discussion about what they did well and where they can improve, and they are

thanked for their efforts. Meanwhile a dozen other such assignments are given out to other work pairs. At first this will seem odd, but within six months you will have the foundational base you need for a highly effective, motivated Evolutionary Team culture. Within three months you can begin asking teams of four and six to do the same thing on a larger scale.

- **Step 2:** Create a Charter for the larger cross-functional team that clearly defines the strategic objective this team will be responsible for executing. In a perfect world, people would volunteer and apply to be on the team and would be tested or auditioned for the team. The participants would both volunteer for and earn their right to be on the team. That's in a perfect world. We know that cannot always happen.

- **Step 3:** Form the team. There are hundreds of books dedicated just to this topic alone — project teams. There are also hundreds of processes for forming project teams. We recommend you read them and choose a process best for your organization. But, to get you started, here are some of our most basic guidelines for selecting team members and forming an Evolutionary Team:

  o   Don't choose all managers or supervisors (this is a classic mistake).
  o   Have at least three departments represented on the team.

- o Limit the size of the team to the size of the work. The best teams are five to fifteen people.
- o Unless you are going to fundamentally change a person's job to be solely the work of the team, ask people to serve for only 90 days at a time.
- o Give the team space and time to work on the project.
- o Team members should end each meeting establishing clarity for what needs to be done and how the team will communicate those ongoing efforts with the rest of the organization. Like all good teams they will speak with "one voice."
- o The team should make progress presentations to senior leaders on a regular basis.
- o The team should have a team sponsor that is a senior leader in the organization, and a team leader.

- **Step 4:** Identify milestones and key performance indicators that the team will use to measure progress and develop a project plan.

- **Step 5:** End the project on a fixed calendar date. If the goal has not been accomplished another team must be ready to take over and the first team will need to account for their failure.

The team becomes Evolutionary when a strategic organizational goal is accomplished and transformational change occurs, but it's so seamless that no one really knows how it happened or whom to thank. Much like the SEAL teams, success often means that the bomb did not go off, the hostage came home or the evil dictator is dead. The outcome is what is noticed, but the team is in the background. The Evolutionary team **chooses** to go to the moon and getting there is the reward. The whole world benefited from the science these remarkable NASA teams created, but no one remembers their names.

===============================

SPECIAL NOTE

Captain Ahlberg warns us that most projects in organizations are executed by "work groups" that we mistakenly call teams. Teams are much more than work groups. We believe that work groups become truly Evolutionary when they transform into real teams. So, you must give the group you choose permission to become a **team**. This means they need the special training, time, and resources to develop a culture *in and of themselves*. That's why you also must let the team stand down at the end date. Where work groups can go on and on, teams need to have an end – just as great sports teams have a "season" and a down time, so do your elite Evolutionary teams need to have a cycle of life.

===============================

CHAPTER 6: EVOLUTIONARY INNOVATION

Innovation. It's buzz word number one in business today. Everyone wants it. But it remains mysterious and elusive. It is the rare company indeed that can consistently innovate and transform. How do Evolutionaries get new ideas? There is no formula or specific science for being innovative. Our friend Chandra Brown, our nation's current Deputy Assistant Secretary of Commerce for Manufacturing and former CEO of United Streetcar tells us that: *"Finding the next big thing is really about synthesizing a lot of different data input from a wide variety of sources—I read a ton—trade reports, fiction, poetry, you name it. I travel. I listen to people. It's priceless to be in a place where people will come to you with new ideas. I see my role as always being open and available to take that call – pretty much anyone can call me with an idea and I will listen to them – most of them probably won't work and are outlandish and outrageous, but the conversation helps frame the constant data input to keep working on synthesizing and predicting where emerging markets will be."*

The real essence of the Evolutionary Innovator is a strong appetite for gathering a wide variety of information from a wide variety of sources. And at the source of all of this information gathering is Bluetooth SIG's commitment to the consumer experience. The Evolutionary Innovator sees his or her job as one of constantly working to gain and refine "perspective." It is not just about doing your job right; Evolutionary Innovators believe it's really about raising the bar on what the whole potential of what your business is and what it can be.

Most businesses fail at innovation because of a misguided effort to preserve their legacy. It's not that organizational commitment to building a strong legacy is a bad thing – in fact it is essential to preserve institutional knowledge and culture. But when we become too focused on preserving legacy at the expense of exploring new ideas and taking calculated risks, we pay the price in loss of innovation. You need Evolutionary Innovators to help you look forward. Innovation is about looking forward but not at the expense of your past. And because it is a part of the Evolutionaries' nature to attach themselves to organizations with a culture and mission they believe in, the Evolutionary Innovator will guide your vision toward innovation while honoring the legacy that exists. It may sound simple, but in practice balancing with one foot in legacy and one foot in innovation is a rare ability for most executives.

HOW EVOLUTIONARIES INNOVATE

Evolutionary Innovators are willing to place bets when it counts and have confidence in themselves and their teams. Sure, sometimes you will invest a significant amount of time and resources into trying a new line of business and it will be a failure. And that failure will often be public. But Evolutionary Innovators know how to look beyond failure for the opportunity on the horizon. They learn from mistakes and apply those lessons to new endeavors. They don't give up, they know how to overcome failure and they don't let fear of the unknown keep them from trying new things, prototyping possibilities, and pushing the envelope ever further.

Evolutionary Innovators:

- **Cast a wide net**
- **Are known as prototypers**
- **Are willing to be uncomfortable**
- **Take a leap of faith**

Chandra Brown tells us that when it comes to predicting future trends and making business decisions that are gutsy and often profitable, she *casts a wide net* for information. She explores avenues of data, conversation, and experience that most leaders would never dream of doing. Chandra is not just reading *Iron Worker Weekly* (we don't know if that is a real magazine, but if it is we are sure she reads it!). Her story teaches us that leaders have an obligation to be fully engaged with a whole range of ideas, people and subjects. We deal with executives all the time in our consulting work, and while they are experts in their industries, they are also unbelievably myopic in their leadership. They often feel like if they are not reading something about their specific business then they are not doing their job. Chandra's success is found in her ability to cast her net well beyond her own industry for new ideas and strategies that put her business one step ahead of the competition.

So, Evolutionary Innovation is fundamentally about how widely you cast your net. The more you read, the more people you talk with, the more industries you study, the more you take in, the more likely you are to get the next great idea. Seeking out this wide variety of information comes naturally to Evolutionaries, especially Bonding Evolutionary Communicators as they are already interested in everyone they meet and every experience they encounter. Evolutionaries naturally possess a healthy curiosity, so casting the net and "catching butterflies" is just a way of life for them.

Evolutionary Innovators are also **known as prototypers**. There is a "word on the street" that you can bring them new ideas and they will give you their ear. They ensure that they will always be the first to hear the next great idea by committing themselves to listening to hundreds of not-so-great ideas. Evolutionary Innovators know that it is impossible for them to be the source of all the good ideas, so they build a reputation for being willing to prototype things for others. They market themselves as "doers" and that invites ideas in. Maybe one in a thousand is great, but ensuring that you see hundreds of ideas gives you the best chance of receiving that one great one.

The good news is that prototyping doesn't have to break the bank for your organization. You can build a culture of rapid prototyping simply by lowering the bar on what it means to "give something a try." We are big fans of the book *The Ten Faces of Innovation* by Tom Kelley. In his chapter on prototyping Kelley explains that you can prototype just about everything, as long as you are willing to "not be precious about it." Kelley argues that even the most crude prototypes can predict a successful idea, and the job of organizational leaders is to create an environment where such less-polished prototypes are encouraged. *"The best organizations are those that make it culturally acceptable to show off ideas at their rough, early stages because those are the organizations that see a whole lot more ideas."*

Perhaps the most difficult requirement for an Evolutionary Innovator is that they **are willing to be uncomfortable.** Just think about It – if you are going to cast your net as widely as possible, your level of tolerance for discomfort must be equally up to the task. You will need to be around people who are much different from you, travel to places that are out of your comfort zone, attend events that you "don't like" (such as NASCAR, or the opera – OK maybe that's just us). In order to bond with new friends you will have to try food that scares you (that sea urchin sushi you think is weird). You will have to constantly push yourself to experience the new and foreign to keep your mind sharp and alive and to remember what it means to do something for the first time. Evolutionary Innovators regularly challenge their biases in life, because they know that this will train them to be more agile and open to innovative opportunities when they arise.

Finally, Evolutionary Innovators are **willing to take leaps of faith.** There is a time and place in great rock climbing where you have to let go of your hand- and footholds at the same time to get to the next place. It's called the "dynamic move" and it is so dramatic that it feels crazy. But it is the only way to move forward and make progress. You don't actually have to take the risk – but it is the only way you can get to the top. Evolutionary Innovators are willing to take risks to achieve progress – to evolve. They make big bets. But just like the climber, they will do everything possible to prepare for that bold move and plan for making it.

And this leap of faith is not just something that happens at the beginning of the transformational change in an organization. Evolutionary Innovators know that as the change efforts around implementing innovation progress, faith will be tested again. This is because for most big efforts, the organization and its people are making a substantial investment of time, money, resources, and opportunity cost. Over time, leaders expect the cost to go down, and ROI (real tangible results) to go up. But there is a time in all such efforts where we find that we have made the investment and there are no real results. This is when all the doubt emerges about why/how we made the original investment in the first place. Even true Evolutionary believers begin to doubt; "did we get the right vendor?" "Are we making the right assumptions?" "What if we are wrong?" We call this progression the Zone of Doubt and Blame.

Evolutionary Innovators are prepared for this Zone – they know it will happen and they know it will take another leap of faith to push through it. But that is the trick – to push through the zone. The key is being able to be bone-level clear about what you are doing and why you are doing it and repeat that message again and again through the zone.

Welcome to the zone

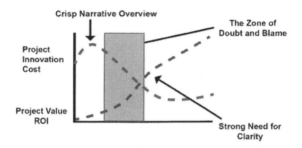

====================================

EVOLUTIONARY INNOVATION IN THE MODERN WORLD

Evolutionary Innovators are constantly playing at the edges of spheres where the game can be changed. Technology, science, medicine. They will gravitate to places where revolutionary innovations have the most chance to transform the world and the way we live, work and build communities. Sure, you could revolutionize accounting principles, but it is unlikely to change the world as we know it. So you will likely find fewer Evolutionaries pursuing degrees in accounting than in digital advertising or foreign policy. And Evolutionaries are often particularly enthralled with technology. They are often accused of chasing "shiny" things – new trends, fads, and games. They are known as early adopters (and sometimes also as early discarders when the next shiny object comes along). But there has to be a little bit of "geek" in every evolutionary. You don't have to be "in" these industries, but you do have to be attracted to these areas in a way that people might perceive as "nerdiness."

====================================

CHAPTER 7: EVOLUTIONARY GUIDANCE

By now it should be very clear that Evolutionaries are always going to be found at the center of high-change dynamic situations. And in modern business, that often looks and feels like chaos. You don't need to look far to find the culprit for the chaos. The vast majority of the time you need only look to the integrity (or lack of integrity) in the planning process. Confusion and chaos are rooted in the inability to realize that planning, execution and assessment are iterative not linear. The role of an Evolutionary in a high-change situation is to act as a shock absorber to all of the incidental actions that could throw your plan off course. We observe that people will identify themselves as either "planners" or "doers." The Evolutionary Guide has the unique ability to *plan while doing* – to reflect and adjust while also in action. The pace of digital business does not tolerate inflexible and static plans. So, Evolutionary Guides are a welcome resource to lead a developmental strategic conversation that may be made up of all kinds of plans and sub-plans.

In this chapter we explore the potential of the Evolutionary Guide. Our experience confirms that organizations that are experiencing high rates of change often show lots of symptoms of stress and dysfunction. Some organizations however seem to be able to exist in a constant state of change and thrive. What's the difference? In a word, the difference is vision. Vision is generally the domain of Senior Leadership and the Board of Directors. The first defining characteristic of Evolutionary Guides is that they get the vision. So when we talk about Evolutionary Guides, we are necessarily talking about your organization's vision and the planning process you use to make your vision real. This is a great chapter for Boards but it is also relevant for anyone who has ever tried to develop, write, socialize or execute a plan. If vision is an essential element in the big picture, guidance is the essential element in realizing that vision. Every plan needs a guide.

Guidance in its broadest definition is everything from advice and counsel to education and psychological support. The best guides, whether leading a whitewater rapids rafting trip, a climb up Mount Kilimanjaro, or a vision quest, are those that do not just guide the course, but the **conduct** expected while traveling that course. Those are the guides that do more than get us from point A to point B, they change us for the better along the way.

The first thing Evolutionary Guides do is include everyone in the planning process. Now, we are not saying that you need to invite every employee into your next planning session! But Evolutionary Guides are always thinking about new and creative ways to plan that allow the people of the organization to "put their fingerprints" on the plan. Sometimes this looks like creating a higher level plan and assigning "sub-plans" to elite teams within the organization to work on for execution strategies. Sometimes it looks like employee surveys and focus groups prior to the planning process. Whatever approach you choose, the key is to be as inclusive as possible.

Often it is the Board of Directors that serves as the "steward of the strategy" for an organization. There is really nothing more "medieval" or arcane than a Board of Directors. But on another level it is really a classic and powerful idea because the potential of a Board is profound – as we know the power of good groups to accomplish good things. And often what we see is that the Board is one of the potential choke points in an organization's ability to really reach its potential. It may be that the Board can be too conservative or too demanding or too aggressive. But the pivotal point here is that the Board is not a neutral party in driving the strategy and the success of Evolutionaries throughout the organization.

So what is the key element of a Board that will be Evolutionary-friendly as opposed to the Board that will choke the Evolutionary potential of a company? The answer is the time horizon of the strategic vision. We believe that Boards become truly Evolutionary when they begin looking out a long way – 10 to 20 years or, in some rare cases, even longer. And the more the Board can define that environment long term, the better Evolutionaries driving long-term change in the organization can be successful.

Evolutionary Boards offer the kind of guidance that constantly identifies and describes the transformative goal and can stay focused on it over years. They are willing to apply resources to it over years, and hold leaders accountable to it over years. And they are confident enough in this vision and its possibility that they are trusted by the organization to operate in the guidance role. Great guidance garners trust. And when organizations trust their Board, amazing things begin to happen.

But we must warn you – if you have an Evolutionary Leader on your Board, this person will likely drive the group crazy! They will always be pushing out to the edge of what is possible. And this may not always be the right course.

Boards that are Evolutionary must commit to bold but long-term visions for long periods of time, and individual Evolutionary members may not have the discipline that the collective needs. It's in the individual Evolutionary Leader's nature to go ranging for new paths. You are glad they have these awesome skills, but they should not always be put to use. Just as we want to have an airline pilot that is capable of doing all sorts of skills maneuvers and impressive feats, we don't want them to do those maneuvers when we are on a plane with our family heading to Hawaii for vacation. Just because you are capable of doing something does not mean your job is to do it all the time. You may want Evolutionary Leaders guiding your vision precisely because they can adapt and excel in disruptive times, but once a vision is established, pressing for change is not appropriate. At some point, guidance is about establishing a vision – and it can be an audacious vision – and sticking to that vision over the long term, even when it loses its luster and becomes boring to the Evolutionary Guides that first envisioned it.

HOW EVOLUTIONARIES GUIDE

Chandra Brown tells us *"there is no formula for good guidance, you are making a reasoned judgment as a human being and so often we shirk that in lieu of trying to create a system for decisions."* This pinpoints the tension in any business that is trying to grow and innovate while also maintaining quality and consistency. We see Boards do this all the time. In an attempt to scale and grow what the organization does well, they mandate that management design and impose "cookie-cutter" processes like job descriptions, technical procedures, and a myriad of systems that are fundamentally designed to remove judgment from the equation in any given situation. And this goal extends to the Board themselves as they begin to write more and more policies designed to remove all judgment from even the highest level of operating the strategy. But, at its heart, guidance is all about judgment.

Evolutionary Boards understand that the function of a truly great strategy is to push guidance down through the organization as a universal competency. The strategy serves as the guide – it provides a lens through which good judgment can be made, without constraining it with too many pre-defined decisioning mechanisms.

Evolutionary Guides:

- *Bring calm to chaos*
- *Know their own minds*
- *Are masters of subtle course correction*
- *Have no predetermined definition of success*

Plans are designed. The team begins execution – excited about the goals ahead. And then the wheels come off the plan (and most likely there is a point where they will). It's in these times that your organization's Evolutionary Guides step in to **bring calm to chaos.** Your organization is better prepared to adapt and flex the plan to meet those changes, because those executing the plan know the plan well – and they also know how to plan well, because you have educated them through the process. And Evolutionary Guides have faith in the team to respond to new scenarios and are able to remain calm.

Evolutionary Guides are able to remain calm and confident in their decisions, even when those decisions are tested, because they **know their own minds.** They are "centered" – they know who they are and what they are about in this world. (This is not to say that they aren't aware of external inputs and are insensitive to the feelings and opinions of those around them, and it is not to say that they know everything or have all the answers, but instead that they have a deep understanding of who they are and it is this confidence that allows them to effectively guide others.) Imagine a snorkeling expedition where a group of tourists sets out with a seasoned local guide to explore the aquatic world. The ocean is a big and mysterious place, as full of danger as it is of wonders. So, even if you are Michael Phelps, you are going to be wearing a life vest. This journey requires more than just expertise, skill and knowledge – the ocean is a complex and nuanced, ever-shifting environment and the guide is there to speak to how to "be" in that world. Again, it's something beyond advice; it's a matter of conduct. It's that ability to be "of the ocean" that makes him or her the *trusted guide* that people follow. Evolutionary Guides have to have more than just expertise, skill and knowledge. They need to be "of the environment" at hand to really guide the organization in it. They must have supreme confidence and security in their own ability on the journey – they have no need to "show off" or demonstrate their prowess unnecessarily. They know that the journey is not about them, but about those they are guiding.

Evolutionary Guides also **are masters of subtle course correction.** They have the ability to offer a constant stream of course-correcting adjustments that are subtle and never make people feel stupid, or humiliate anyone, or are designed to "show off" their own expertise. Evolutionary Guides have good judgment. They see more, they hear more, and they can make reasoned decisions. For this reason, Evolutionary Guides are rarely surprised. They are aware of the surrounding and dynamics of a journey and are not afraid to make decisions with lack of data or limited time. Judgment occurs routinely and consistently with obviously held and relevant values. This sort of quiet and reassuring confidence is the reflection of "being of" their environment.

Perhaps the most important characteristic of Evolutionary Guides is that they have no **predetermined definition of success** around the journey. They are open-minded about how a challenge can be met effectively, the paths available to success, and what a winning strategy might be. This is harder to do than it sounds. The balance between offering sound judgment and also remaining open to unexplored possibilities is a delicate one to master. Evolutionary Guides also make no predetermined judgment about which team members are going to take the lead on the journey. Just as on a trail hike unexpected leaders may emerge, the same will be true in your organization. Transformative change is inherently disruptive, and as your organization becomes less stable, moving through the change, new leaders – Evolutionary leaders – will rise to the surface. They may not be the people you expect. They may not hold official leadership titles in the company. But they will be the ones you need. Evolutionary Guides are quick to recognize these people and make space for them to take the lead for the success of the journey.

So what does this mean for developing a high-performance Evolutionary Board? It means that the single most important role for the Board is to anticipate and plan for significant changes, both internal and external, that the organization will face. Think of it as "reading the rapids." The digital business environment is unforgiving if you are unable to operate at a very fast tempo. Evolutionary Boards do two things: they trust and empower their Senior Management to handle the day-to-day, month-to-month "paddling" through the rapids, and they are always working to get a better view of what's coming up. Ironically, we believe that the digital tempo of business demands a longer view of the future and we reject the idea that "because everything is changing so fast we can't make a plan." Evolutionary Boards have figured out how to bring powerful intelligence from other guides into the boardroom. They are quick to hike downstream themselves (by looking at other organizations, attending appropriate conferences, commissioning research, etc.) to see what the future holds. Their plans both react to their assessment of the future and most importantly take control of that future. They put the organization in a fundamentally proactive and offensive position. This difference is felt all through the organization. There are huge implications for efficiency, quality, recruitment and morale. When the people in an organization know that they have a strong guiding body they can rely on, they are able to focus on the mission and are able to unfold their complete potential. If on a long hike you can trust that your guide is navigating well, you are free to concentrate on each step, optimizing your own performance and even helping those around you succeed.

We can't stress enough that Boards and Senior Leadership Teams frequently and dramatically underestimate their actual power and influence. Just as we cannot *not* communicate, people in leadership positions cannot *not* lead. Evolutionary Guides know that everything they do is being understood as an act of guidance.

CHAPTER 8: EVOLUTIONARY WOMEN

Over the last decade of consulting we have had the opportunity to work with several women who are highly developed Evolutionaries. And while they have found their way to an authentic and confident approach to the transformational change efforts they lead, many have shared the feeling of pressure to be something different than who they really were in order to succeed in their careers. For this reason, we couldn't finish this book without exploring the question: "Why do highly competent executive women come to believe that they need to change who they are in order to achieve levels of top leadership?"

There is an old joke used frequently in Human Resources circles: "Mobile technology is the most disruptive thing to happen to the workplace since women entered it in the 1940s!" Since women entered the workforce, they have come a long way. Today girls outnumber boys in high school graduation rates, college enrollment, and school leadership positions. In 2010 more women were employed in our country than men for the first time in history. And while some may say the progress has been and continues to be too slow, women are now in line for CEO positions across the nation. Many of these women are Evolutionaries. They have had to be to get where they are! Breaking new ground in their industries and to be the "first" as women in their leadership roles requires a certain degree of Evolutionary prowess.

Executive coach and CEO of The Link for Women, Cindy Tortorici tells us that: *"Most of the women I talk to in senior executive positions feel lonely. There are very few women in the arena to begin with, so finding a mentor, a colleague, a coach, a friend can be difficult. And, unlike men in these positions, there is no built-in culture because we are still too new to the game."*

Often the reason women feel, once promoted to C-suite positions, that they need a "personality transplant" in order to succeed is because there is no example around them of how to be a woman in these roles. But times continue to evolve, and Evolutionary women are paving the way for those to come – transforming the role of executive, CEO, and their organizations in the process.

Chandra Brown shares her story: *"As a woman in a male-dominated business, when I walk into a room I usually stand out. I may be the only woman in the room or I may be the youngest person in the room but I think it is fantastic because when I make a point everyone will remember that point because of who delivered it. So you can look at it as a difficulty or as a negative but I look at it very much as strength. It can be a huge strategic advantage as you move forward."*

Many times when women engage in assertive behaviors such as those Chandra encourages, they are tagged with labels like "dragon lady," "domineering" or even just "mean." There is no question that Chandra is smart, driven, and ambitious. But ambition in a woman often carries negative connotations in our society. Chandra embraces her aggressive side as a strength – one aspect of what has helped her to be a successful and nationally respected leader in innovation and manufacturing today. Evolutionary women like Chandra have a lot to teach us about transformative change, courage and tenacity. And there are good financial reasons for organizations to pay attention to what they have to say.

WHY YOU NEED EVOLUTIONARY WOMEN

In their book *Womenomics*, Claire Shipman and Katty Kay shocked the business world with a mountain of data proving that "putting women in charge is good for a company's bottom line." Studies conducted in nearly 200 of the Fortune 500 companies concluded that those organizations that were better at promoting women to senior positions experienced higher returns than those that did not. A series of studies documented in the book indicated that women executives in top management were better at promoting teamwork, motivating employees and fostering a creative environment. All of which are essential in fast-paced, innovative companies desiring transformative change. Evolutionary women are more willing to step into these roles, to be the "first" among their peers to hold these positions, and are most likely to put a "higher cause" at the center of their work over personal ambition and rewards.

And these benefits translate to placing Evolutionary women on Boards of Directors as well. Research organizations Catalyst and McKinsey & Company have pioneered research linking gender balance and Board performance, showing that Boards with three or more women gained a significant

100

performance edge over the competition, including 73% return on sales, 83% return on equity and 112% return on invested capital. Other aspects of the study show that when women have a strong representation on Senior Executive Teams those companies exceed peers in nine different performance criteria. This is not a book about data — but it's hard to ignore these and hundreds of other studies producing statistics that are nothing short of astonishing.

By now you are probably thinking, "OK, so if placing women at a senior level is so good for an organization's financial bottom line, why don't we see more women in these positions? Why isn't everyone promoting them?" Well, first, these women are tough. Evolutionary women are smart, no-nonsense, and quick to reject the business-as-usual cultural expectations that can arise from decades of "good-ol'-boy" management practices. Second, they are, for the most part, fed up with the status quo and looking for ways to work better, smarter, and with more integrity. They keep score differently. They measure success differently. In short, they are bound to shake things up a bit just by virtue of being different. It's not that there is a shortage of great talent in the pool — over 50% of middle level managers are women. So if you are still reading this, and your company is in need of transformational change and an increase in profitability, recruit a few Evolutionary women.

Evolutionary Women:

- *Are willing to be the first*
- *Establish credibility early and often*
- *Build a network of other Evolutionary Women*
- *Dream big*

One of the most courageous qualities that Evolutionary women possess is that they *are willing to be first.* Most of these women are pioneers in workplace domains long dominated by men – political office, corporate executive suites, boards of directors, medicine, technology, consulting, law and more. They are ready to cope with the loneliness they will feel as they spend most of their time with groups of men, and find that the occasional women they come across also view them as "set apart" because of the unconventional career choices that Evolutionary women tend to make.

Evolutionary women know that they are an exception to the norm when it comes to their position and behavior in the business environment. So, they accept that they will need to *establish their credibility early and often* in their careers. They will need to prove their credibility every time they meet someone new. That may not be fair, but it's a fact of life for them. They learn not to take it personally, and they just do it. They are resigned to the idea of proving themselves over and over again. They become very good at talking about what they do and why it matters. They know how to talk about ideas with enthusiasm and how to energize the people around them. They are not afraid to bring their passion and energy to the table, knowing that that combination of conviction and passion with the right data and evidence is the magic formula for bringing people along with them in their mission.

And they are authentic. They are constantly battling that voice in their heads that says, "For this job, you will have to change your personality." Too many women in business feel that they need to change themselves in order to fit in. Because Evolutionary women have come to peace with the idea of being more isolated than those around them, they are able to hold onto who they really are. This doesn't mean that Evolutionary women no longer care about relationships. Like any Evolutionary, they see relationships as paramount. But they accept that they may never be completely understood by the people they work with. They will have to find their support system somewhere else. Which leads us to our next point.

Evolutionary women know that they need to *build a network of other Evolutionary women*. They quickly learn that the key to hanging onto who you are is to find people that are trying to do the same sorts of Evolutionary things in the world and build a connection with them. Cindy Tortorici tells us that once women get to a senior level they are expected to shift from being task-oriented superstars to visionary strategists. But they don't have the same access as men to networks where the rules of the game are explained as a matter of course. So Evolutionary women are proactive – they seek out other women who have taken this journey before them (but are likely in another industry or organization) and ask them for their wisdom.

This desire to connect to other Evolutionary women is not just driven by the need to hold onto self, it is the only way to truly accomplish the kind of goals that real Evolutionaries aspire to – changing the world. Influential people have influential networks. People don't get much done by themselves, no matter how smart and powerful they are. Evolutionary women know that they are going to need to build coalitions of other women with common goals in order to get things done. And this connects to the fundamental Evolutionary concept that "it's not about you" – that there is a larger community that you are responsible to and for in your work and in your life.

Finally, Evolutionary women **_dream big._** They are optimistic, future-oriented and willing to navigate through a lot of disparity, unfairness, and doubt to see their transformational visions come to life. At heart, all Evolutionaries are dreamers. Thinking big is just a part of who they are. It's in their DNA.

In her book *The Curse of the Good Girl,* Rachel Simmons laments that girls in the United States are incredibly high performers, collecting "achievements by the handful" in school, but often don' t have the confidence to own them. She tells us that young women are consistently outpacing young men in academic programs, but continue to represent only a third of business school students and a quarter of law-firm partners. "If you look at girls on paper, they're terrific," says Simmons, but that performance is not translating into the leadership sphere as adults.

Evolutionary women are not born Evolutionary. They are a product of their own hard work, combined with talent sets, mentoring, opportunities, and an environment conducive to developing Evolutionary potential. The most future-thinking Evolutionary women are investing in the next generation, encouraging these high-achieving girls to chase their dreams.

Final Note: All of our Evolutionary characteristics in this book are consistent with the principles of androgyny that assume no person is beholden to a set of archetypical behavior that limits them. The androgynous person is successful in more situations because he or she doesn't have to adhere to a role that is solely masculine or feminine. It's not gender-neutral, but it is not gender-*constrained*. In other words, to be an Evolutionary is to be adaptable to the needs of a given transformative challenge, regardless of the masculine or feminine characterization of those necessary behaviors.

So, whether you believe that Evolutionary women are just "acting like men" or that they truly bring something unique and valuable to the game, the point is this:

1) We need to promote more women to leadership positions – if not because it is the *right* thing to do, then simply because it is the *effective* and *profitable* thing to do.

2) Evolutionary women, especially those who have "made it," need support networks beyond what most current male-dominated leadership teams can provide. They should be encouraged and supported in these efforts.

CHAPTER 9: THE CODE OF AN EVOLUTIONARY

Realized Evolutionaries are rare. Many people have some of the qualities, but not all of them. We estimate that maybe five out of a thousand people are true Evolutionaries. That is one of the reasons why the Evolutionary code is so important. The self-aware Evolutionary has a huge amount of power, and that should mean that they also have a huge level of responsibility – a code of conduct that guides them.

The cornerstone of the code is a commitment to a cause that is larger than the individual. The pursuit of personal excellence is always in some fashion at the **service** of that larger cause. This larger cause is rooted in making the world a better place – leaving a positive and healthy legacy for generations to come. Evolutionaries understand that there is very little in this world of value that has not been created on the leveraged power of strong relationships between people. It takes teams to get most of the great work of the world done. We are interconnected, and those connections must be fundamentally understood and honored – and Evolutionaries know that this core relationship-building is the key to achieving truly great and lasting outcomes.

If you have read this book to this point and you find yourself resonating with the ideas that we have shared, and if you have found yourself nodding in agreement, or saying, "Finally, someone gets the way I feel!" then you may in fact be an Evolutionary. Chances are that you feel misunderstood by a lot of people. Chances are you resent it when people look at one of your actions and trivialize the reason for it. If you really want to upset an Evolutionary, question their motives. Because that is the whole point for an Evolutionary – *why* you are doing something is a very big deal!

THE EVOLUTIONARY CODE: WE KNOW WHY

This simple statement holds a lot of meaning. It means that you may be following, but you are not following blindly. You may be leading, but you are not driven by ego. You know why you are doing what you are doing and why it matters for a larger cause. You may find yourself with multiple layers of motives that are in play in a given situation or job, but there is an integrity at the foundation of all of those motives. They are driven by the pursuit of a set of positive values.

Evolutionaries may even feel like it is not worth the effort to do something unless several positive values are achieved at one time. Evolutionaries are looking for ways to create ecosystems of positive change that reinforce each other.

We Know Why means exercising your best judgment at any given moment. You cannot put a formula on how that judgment works, but if you make poor choices, you need to ask yourself how could you have judged better in that situation? What can you do to better inform your judgment as you evolve?

So what are the characteristics of Evolutionaries that follow the code?

Realized Evolutionaries are:

1. *Deeply compassionate*
2. *Transparent*
3. *Courageous*
4. *Trustworthy*
5. *Committed to excellence as a form of SERVICE*
6. *Legacy-minded*

You cannot be a true Evolutionary and not be **deeply compassionate.** Evolutionaries are not ashamed of the compassion they carry into every situation they encounter. We are not saying that all Evolutionaries are Mother Teresa (though she certainly was an Evolutionary), but all Evolutionaries do genuinely care about other people and about the future we leave for the next generation. Put simply, you cannot be aloof to suffering and be an Evolutionary.

Evolutionaries know that a **transparent** motive is the key for being an effective influencer. If the motive is pure and people can see that about you, you will naturally begin to garner followers. Transparent leadership is another hot buzz word in business today. Transparency tends to be a term used to talk about sharing documents, conducting open meetings, and including as many people as possible in every decision. But all of these things are just a Band-Aid on a cancer – the real issue is that we don't trust the motives of the people running Wall Street, the people on Capitol Hill, and the people reporting our news. Real transparency is about laying your motive on the table, doing the right thing, and following through on your promises – something realized Evolutionaries do every day.

Evolutionaries live by a simple rule of thumb: If it's tough, it is probably the right thing to do. And doing the right thing is almost always a *courageous* act. Evolutionaries know that transformative experience is almost never about making things easy or simple, it is about fighting the dragons of complexity and not giving up – a sort of resolute approach, a willingness to take hits, to fail, to take risks, to offer personal sacrifice and abandon old rules in order to further the cause – even if that cause can't be fully accomplished in one's lifetime.

Evolutionaries are *trustworthy.* It's as simple as that. Evolutionaries are people that you would trust with your pocketbook and your children as well as your business. It's not that they are perfect. They might make a mistake, but they would tell you they made it, how they made it, and what they learned from it. Because they are comfortable with who they are, confident in their values, and unafraid of showing their "authentic selves" to the world, Evolutionaries are trusted individuals. Because they are compassionate and able to think beyond themselves and their own self-interests, people can believe in them. They keep their promises and they honor their commitments. You will often see Evolutionaries in long-term committed relationships. They view trust as a matter of honor.

In our company, we live and breathe the mantra that "there is no substitute for personal excellence." Evolutionaries are no strangers to the pursuit of greatness. They will strive for years to master competencies they believe are important. But unlike the individual that pursues excellence for the sake of excellence, Evolutionaries are **committed to excellence as a form of SERVICE.** Evolutionaries understand that the most important work of their lifetime will be realized in the context of fulfilled potential – their own and the potential of those that they teach, coach, and lead. Evolutionaries have no set level of expectations for what "success" is. Instead, by *realized potential*, we mean that Evolutionaries recognize that some people can give more than others, learn more than others, bear more weight than others, are simply capable of more than those around them. So they don't have preconceived notions of what it means to be excellent – the point is that the more you are capable of, the more you should do. Evolutionaries know they are capable of a great deal. And so they hold themselves to a higher standard.

But, while the Evolutionary may achieve great status in his or her career, the relationship to another person is never optimized from the consideration of being "one up" or "one down" in any regard. They are not keeping score. That does not mean an Evolutionary won't tell you what to do or that an Evolutionary can't be told what to do, but it means that the score keeping is not a feature of the relationship. It's about being fiercely committed to excellence *and at the same* time not interested in who is better than whom. This is a rare blend. Many people are committed to excellence but also keep score. And many people don't keep score, but also don't aspire to achieve. Evolutionaries are able to achieve excellence while not keeping score, because competition with others is not what drives the Realized Evolutionary. The downside to this is that Evolutionaries may not always give recognition as well as they should, because they themselves are not in as much need of it.

Evolutionaries live in the future. They are *legacy-minded* in the way they approach their work and their life. They have both the ability to and desire to think in future-oriented terms. Evolutionaries care about the future, their participation in it and how they can best use their individual potential to make the world a better place through the work that they contribute in their lifetime. The Evolutionary has a responsibility to people younger and people older than them. They are conscious of the generational nature of life and are willing and able to adapt their messaging to each generation. Evolutionaries are acutely aware that we reap what we sow, and have a sensibility for making an investment – they know that as the generation before us did for us, we do now for them. Evolutionary people really do think several generations down the road. They think in terms of the legacy of an organization or community. They are very comfortable thinking outside of their own life span. They see the work they do almost as a part of a great relay race – this life is about running only one leg – what will you do with the baton in the very short time that you have it before you have to pass it on to the next teammate? To look generations backward and generations ahead is a point of maturity as an Evolutionary. You will recall from Chapter 1 of this book that there are degrees of Evolutionaries. It is only in the level of mastery that Evolutionaries truly understand the way in which their lifetime is just one very small part of the story that they are playing a role in. Only at the ultimate achievement – mastery – do we realize how small we actually are.

MAKING MAGIC: When people are obviously living by the Code of the Evolutionary, they are attracted to and attractive to others who are also living the code. So, by living the Code, you gain access to whole networks of Evolutionary people who are also trying to change the world for the better in core ways. And they are also willing to help each other, share ideas, explore opportunities, and invest in communities. These networks create the Evolutionary ecosystems that can facilitate the kind of good work that those around us often label as a "miracle" or "magic." People will often look at an event, new idea or altruistic community activism and say, "How did that happen?" It happens through the phenomenal informal networks of people who openly and proudly share a Code that drives innovation, good work and a beautiful future for generations to come.

CHAPTER 10: WHEN EVOLUTIONARIES FAIL

We have said before in this book that no one would want a whole organization full of Evolutionaries. This sort of lack of balance would mean details are missed, systems are underdeveloped, and procedures inconsistent, just to name a few problems. Because Evolutionaries are inherently collaborative, they often reveal plans or visions before they are fully baked and those plans are destroyed by the potentially well-meaning but nay-saying "realists" that surround them. Evolutionaries often do not realize that there is a lot of lonely work to be done before they can unveil their idea to others. The assumption that others will want to be a part of a ground-floor collaboration, and that they will want to work through the options and problem-solve an idea with you, is often a false one. In fact most people simply don't have the capacity, the patience, or the curiosity to spend time exploring something new, so they are hardwired to avoid change.

Evolutionaries can also fail because they are morally opposed to head games and politics – remember, they are the very definition of transparency. And that would work in an ideal world. But the reality of business is that to be successful, sometimes you have to play the political games, offer the favors, and make the questionable compromises. This is not to say that because people are not generally interested in new ideas, and politics often rules the day in any organization, that Evolutionaries would be better off to shut others out. This does not mean that Evolutionaries should abandon their commitment to collaborative dialogue and planning. But the Evolutionary will fail when he or she does not establish the right level of expectation when introducing a new idea. The simple way to say it is: the failed Evolutionary does not recognize the threatening quality of even the most positive suggestion.

Most of the time it is good that people avoid change. Even good change involves a risk; we are hardwired as a human race to avoid risk, so even good change is resisted. This sort of behavior is ingrained in us to preserve us – it's based in all sorts of survival instincts we've had since our race began. But Evolutionaries operate in what Kenneth Burke refers to as a "comic frame" – external inputs and outputs are part and parcel to what they are all about. The unexpected in this frame is just a part of the reality and is often welcomed. "Tragic-framed" people (or, most people) may have real trouble with an Evolutionary. This is a "closed loop" approach to life that constantly screens and rejects inputs that would disrupt the current worldview of the individual. Burke also makes the point that both of these frames are central to the human condition. It is not that one is good and one is bad. But what it does mean is that when an Evolutionary bumps up against a person who has a more dogmatic, black and white view of the universe, there will likely be tension. This tension is also not good or bad. Evolutionaries fail when they are not able to navigate and appreciate the conflict as generative. Instead, they become blocked and defined by the conflict, dismissing information or ideas that may be of value.

Evolutionaries attract followers for a variety of reasons, and those reasons are very important. Evolutionaries fail

114

when they misunderstand or ignore the reasons for which people are following. For example, people may follow an Evolutionary out of sympathy rather than commitment to a cause that is bigger than the individuals involved. If you are sick – physically or emotionally – you will struggle with an Evolutionary dynamic because people will want to take care of you. That's not a bad thing – it can be good to show vulnerability and accept compassion. The realized Evolutionary will leverage the compassion of others to address something larger. If an Evolutionary has cancer, he or she will deflect conversations about his or her own way of dealing with the illness and instead will want to talk about how to eradicate cancer from the world. The way they ask for help is to solve something bigger. But Evolutionaries fail when they are unable to deflect tragedy (or a windfall) and allow it to get in the way of what they know to be the real focus of their life's work. This is not about being a "hero" or being "invincible" – it is at its core a fundamentally human response. It is a response driven by vision, commitment to excellence, the drive to leave a legacy and compassion rather than self-pity or self-obsession. The point is that we are defined as much by the people that follow us as by the vision we pursue. You don't need to look far to find examples of well-intended organizations that are brought down by followers who do not share the standards of integrity established by the leaders. Just as the motive for leadership is integral to successful leadership, the motive of the followers must be in alignment to achieve true Evolutionary change.

Just as we want followers to follow the vision, and not the Evolutionary who created it, Evolutionaries fail when they lead from a place of ego rather than purpose. Just like anyone else, Evolutionaries fail when they drink too much of their own Kool-Aid – when they start to believe it is about them instead of about the work, the organization, the community. When this happens, you are no longer, by definition, an Evolutionary. As you read in the Code of an Evolutionary chapter, there is a need for clarity and diligence to keep the values front and center. It is OK to be personally invested in the transformative change that you are trying to accomplish (Evolutionaries always are) and it is normal to have moments where you temporarily lose sight of the real goal; the trick is to interrupt the delusional thought pattern that puts you in the center of the universe.

Evolutionaries also fail because they underestimate the power of a really good idea and a really good vision. When you look at communities that are achieving truly great things, you almost always wonder, "How did that start? How did that take hold?" One of the best examples of this is the "End Polio" campaign conducted by Rotary International. Twenty-five years ago Rotary, more to the point Rotarians – real people – set out with the audacious goal of eliminating the scourge of polio. Now, we are on the brink of completely eradicating the disease. This achievement went well beyond fundraising to embracing the entire cycle of behavior, medicine, prevention, education and governmental support that would be necessary to end polio. Rotary established a framework that offered a variety of "entry points" for key partners to engage in the effort. This super-powerful vision to change the world flourished precisely because Rotary invited people to participate in a solution and people stepped up. People are looking for these sorts of solutions. They are hungry for it. Scale is a part of what an Evolutionary is all about – making a difference in the world, for the community, for the universe – not just triple bottom lines, but triple *triple* bottom lines – Evolutionaries fail because they don't play on a big enough stage, often because they have been told one too many times that this sort of dream is impossible and they began to listen.

Evolutionaries can also fail because they suffer from the belief, "How hard can it be?" Evolutionaries are notoriously prone to underestimate the complexity of innovative ideas and be overly optimistic in the ability of their team to overcome obstacles. Because they readily see the maximum potential of those around them, they are prone to automatically assume people will naturally fulfill their potential when presented with a problem or a challenge. In fact, this is not the case. Most people never reach their potential. And for this reason, most people surprise Evolutionaries by not "rising to the task" and making the impossible happen. Evolutionaries are devastated by this reality, but never seem to learn from it. They move on eagerly and optimistically to the next new idea, new project, new team and miraculously have the same expectations that the people around them will rise to the occasion and fulfill their maximum potential and change the world together. The Evolutionary keeps believing, though, because every once in a while, people come through. Like a slot machine that pays off just enough to keep you standing there, Evolutionaries find just enough reward in seeing others rise to their highest potential that it confirms their optimism. So yes, Evolutionaries are a little crazy. To avoid failure, Evolutionaries should welcome the view of the pragmatist, the nay-sayer, to keep them grounded and realistic about the capabilities of the talent they lead.

But the number one big reason Evolutionaries fail is because they don't have the discipline and attention span to pick up their good ideas and bring them to fruition. So when their idea is shot down by the team, they are often not ready or able to carry out their idea on their own. They need others to help them make their ideas real, so they need to be able to sell their ideas. This means that Evolutionaries need to get better at baking their ideas more completely before presenting them. And, when you inevitably present your next half-baked idea, and it gets shot down by the realists in the room, see that feedback as a blessing. It shows you the objection you need to prepare for in the next dialogue you pursue.

Finally, beyond the organizational weaknesses that most Evolutionaries possess, there is a genuine Dark Side to the Evolutionary personality. Often Evolutionaries fail because they are too open with their hearts, investing in the potential they see in others, dreaming big, and placing their own reputations on the line. By opening their hearts and minds so widely, by not deflecting or finding unhealthy ways of processing or coping with the intense lives they lead, they often invite deeper pain and heartache than most people can suffer. It is hard to care so much – about so much. Possessing the maturity to deal with (and carry) as much as they do is still an incredible burden. Being a Realized Evolutionary means walking an exhausting and heartbreaking path. But the payoff can be big too – the knowledge that you truly did your best in this life, gave all you had to give, and left the world just a little bit better place for having lived in it for a brief while.

The Evolutionary existence is based on gaining momentum through the accumulation of experience in service and transformation. It is about starting small, but thinking big. If after the previous paragraph you find yourself second-guessing the desirability of the Evolutionary lifestyle, that's OK! What you can do is recognize and support the efforts of the Evolutionaries around you who are driven to walk this path. As you conclude reading this book, you could choose to walk away with a broad, general impression of the potential of being an Evolutionary. Or, you could begin right now identifying specific concepts that inform challenges you are facing right now. You could identify specific questions that came out of your reading that you will take steps to answer. You could begin making incremental changes in your approach to conversations, planning, innovation, leadership and guidance. Or you could simply support the people who do with kind words, small gestures and whatever encouragement you can offer. These simple acts of support are critical for an Evolutionary to achieve transformative change.

CONCLUSION

We think an easy and powerful next step is to have a conversation with someone else who read this book. We think you will be amazed at how different another person's impression of the value and challenge of being or working with an Evolutionary can be. It is especially interesting to hear the point of view of an Evolutionary who has read the book. Our hope in writing this book is that we have created an invitation for people to talk about a worldview that has been hidden in plain sight for generations. For a true Evolutionary the recognition that you are not alone should be liberating and extremely compelling. For those who work and live with Evolutionaries it should be confirming of the opportunities and challenges you face in collaborating with, supporting and loving these rare people.

During the writing of this book we introduced the Evolutionaries term to many of the people we work with. And we are delighted when our clients talk to us about the Evolutionaries in their organizations. They are beginning to see the world differently. As this terminology takes hold, we see our clients developing a whole new view of what is possible, even though they are working with the same staff, the same resources, the same constraints and the same vision. The ability to name it and talk about it gives you the power to do what you could not do before. Language precedes and informs our perception of reality. The language of the Evolutionary experience is in itself transformative — allowing those who speak it to take control.

One more thing about Evolutionaries: they know when to stop pondering and start doing. The book is over. Time to get busy!

About the Authors

Randy Harrington, PhD is CEO and owner of Strategic Arts and Sciences, Extreme Arts and Sciences and Best Practices Media. After completing his doctorate in organizational communication from the University of Oregon in 1992, he began his consulting career. With 25 years of experience, Dr. Harrington is now one of the premier consultants to financial institutions in the USA. He is a sought after strategic planner and executive coach as well as for his work in organizational change management and media messaging. His theories on the effectiveness of high-impact teams and communication push clients like Microsoft, Blue Tooth SIG Inc. and the United Nations to work smarter and more efficiently. Dr. Harrington also earns lots of frequent flier miles—delivering keynote speeches each year to audiences from New York to Kyoto. He is an avid guitarist, cook, and scuba diver. He makes his home in Eugene, Oregon with his wife, Patty.

Carmen E. Voillequé is the co-founder of Strategic Arts and Sciences and the CEO of Best Practices Media. With 20 years of experience in educational psychology and organizational development, Ms. Voillequé is nationally respected for her expertise in strategic planning, organizational change management and implementing high performance teams for project execution. She serves a diverse base of clients in finance, technology, travel & tourism, law, government, non-profit, education, health care and hospitality. Past and current clients include Microsoft, Bluetooth SIG, Travel Oregon, the Federal Judicial Center in Washington D.C., and a variety of credit unions and financial institutions across the country. When not working, she enjoys traveling with her husband and daughter. She and her family make their home in Portland, Oregon.

To experience more Evolutionary stories, visit us at
www.areyouevolutionary.com or
www.strategicartsandsciences.com.

Made in the USA
Lexington, KY
25 January 2017